UNLEASHING GOD'S POWER IN YOU

Neil T. Anderson
& Robert L. Saucy

HARVEST HOUSE PUBLISHERS

EUGENE, OREGON

Cover by Terry Dugan Design, Minneapolis, Minnesota

UNLEASHING GOD'S POWER IN YOU
The Bondage Breaker® Series
Copyright © 2004 by Neil T. Anderson and Robert L. Saucy
Published by Harvest House Publishers
Eugene, Oregon 97402
www.harvesthousepublishers.com

Library of Congress Cataloging-in-Publication Data
Anderson, Neil T., 1942–
   Unleashing God's power in you / Neil T. Anderson and Robert L. Saucy.
      p. cm. — (The bondage breaker series)
   Includes bibliographical references.
   ISBN 0-7369-1442-0 (pbk.)
   1. Holiness.   2. Spiritual life—Christianity.   I. Saucy, Robert L.   II. Title.   III. Series.
   BT767.A53   2004
   234'.8—dc22   2004009667

Printed in the United States of America

04   05   06   07   08   09   10   11   / VP-CF /   10   9   8   7   6   5   4   3   2   1

Acknowledgments and Dedication

Christian books are more than a gathering of information. They are (or they should be) a reflection of one's life. It is essential for our own sanctification that we live what we teach. That is why writing a book on Christian maturity can seem a little presumptuous. Who are we to write a book on holiness? We certainly haven't arrived at any degree of perfection, but we have tried our best to model growth and be a catalyst for what Paul describes as God's will for our lives—that is, our sanctification (1 Thessalonians 4:3).

We have had the privilege of interacting with seminary students and church leaders for many years. We have learned so much from them in the educational process and are grateful for each one of them. They keep us honest and challenge our thinking. We have also learned from each other, with Robert being an idealist and linear thinker, and Neil being a pragmatist and holistic thinker. Hopefully that makes for a better book.

We are grateful to Harvest House Publishers for trusting us with this message on sanctification. Our editor, Paul Gossard, has been especially helpful and insightful. He has been a vital member of this writing team, as has been all the crew at Harvest House.

I (Neil) am deeply indebted to Dr. Saucy. He has been my mentor and friend, and has served on the board of Freedom in Christ Ministries for many years. I count it a great honor to write a book with this highly esteemed professor of systematic theology. For ten years we taught together at Talbot School of Theology. I can attest that he lived what he taught, and I have heard his students say the same.

I can't imagine what Talbot School of Theology will be like without him as he nears retirement. The administration at Biola University has always looked to Dr. Saucy for the divine perspective. He is more than a great mind—he was and is an honest and godly theologian who has earned the respect of his students and colleagues. It is my great privilege to dedicate this book to the man I look up to the most for godly wisdom and integrity. We all love you, Dr. Saucy, and thank God for you.

—Neil T. Anderson

Contents

The Route to a Meaningful Life

*Holiness appeared to me to be of a sweet, pleasant,
charming, serene, calm nature; which brought
an inexpressible purity, brightness, peacefulness,
and ravishment to the soul. In other words,
that it made the soul like a field or garden of God,
with all manner of pleasant flowers.*

JONATHAN EDWARDS

Why should we make the effort to conform to God's image? Is there anything in it for us?

It sounds unrighteous to even ask the question. In popular parlance, *it's all about God*. He is the Potter and we are the clay. However, to say that we as earthen vessels have no value or purpose is to diminish the role of the Potter, and to distort what it means to be created in His image.

To remain a lifeless hunk of clay is the ultimate tragedy. To be molded into something beautiful by the hands of a loving Creator who breathed His life into us is the ultimate value. To come alive but remain shapeless is to rob ourselves of many rich rewards. Scripture makes this promise to those who come to

God believing that He exists: "He is a rewarder of those who seek Him" (Hebrews 11:6 NASB). God wants us to know there are rewards for those who seek Him and want to become all He created us to be. He knew that, without the assurance of some personal benefit, there would be little commitment. So what should motivate us to pursue God and His righteousness, and what is keeping us from fulfilling our calling?

The Wrong Motivation

The command to be holy because God is holy (1 Peter 1:16) has in the past led some religious zealots to a life of asceticism (see definition below) and legalism. Their motivation to obey God and live a righteous life leads them to try to rid themselves of all harmful influences. Such thinking has driven some people to desert monasteries to endure lifestyles of deprivation. That is not very appealing to most of us! Modern forms of asceticism have led to separatism and legalism, the idea being to separate ourselves from all the pleasures and influences of this world. That would make the fulfillment of the great commission a difficult—if not impossible—task! Trying not to sin does not result in righteousness. It often leads to self-righteousness. Instead of loving our neighbor, we sit in judgment of them.

Jesus thundered against such religious hypocrisy—and the apostle Paul warned us about religious asceticism, which is the practice of strict self-denial as a measure of personal and spiritual discipline:

> Let no one keep defrauding you of your prize by delighting in self-abasement...These are matters which have, to be sure, the appearance of wisdom in self-made religion and self-abasement and severe treatment of the body, but are of no value against fleshly indulgence (Colossians 2:18,23 NASB).

Such religious zealots may seem to be "sound in faith," but in reality they are "sour in face," and have made Christianity so unattractive that few are interested.

People can see the hypocrisy of the legalists who try to live up to external standards, and they see no pleasure in an ascetic lifestyle. Have you ever thought, *I can't have fun or enjoy life anymore, because I have to be holy?* How many people in their teens and 20s think that? If that is even remotely your idea of pursuing holiness, you will lack the proper motivation to go further.

The hidden motivation for religious asceticism and legalism is often an irrational fear. Those who lead such lives strive for moral perfection as a means of avoiding punishment. They have a law relationship with a stern, distant, and demanding God, instead of a personal love relationship with their heavenly Father. John shows this when he explains how things should be: "There is no fear in love; but perfect love casts out fear, because fear involves punishment, and the one who fears is not perfected in love" (1 John 4:18 NASB).

True Motivation

Jesus said,

> If anyone wishes to come after Me, he must deny himself, and take up his cross daily and follow Me. For whoever wishes to save his life will lose it but whoever loses his life for My sake, he is the one who will save it. For what is a man profited if he gains the whole world, and loses or forfeits himself? (Luke 9:23-25 NASB).

It seems rather austere, doesn't it? We are supposed to sell ourselves out for God with very little to gain for our efforts. Nothing could be further from the truth, though.

The middle sentence in the above quote is a play on words. People who seek to find their identity, purpose, and meaning in their physical, natural, and temporal existence will eventually lose it all. No matter how many toys and trophies we accumulate in the span of our natural life, we can't take it with us. However, those who find new life in Christ will keep it for all eternity. Denying yourself is denying self-rule and acknowledging God as your Creator and Lord. It may seem sacrificial, but what are you actually sacrificing?

Some Sacrifice!

You are sacrificing the lower life to gain the higher life. (Why people choose to be happy as animals instead of being blessed as children of God is the mystery of the ages and reveals our lack of understanding.)

You are sacrificing the pleasure of things to gain the pleasure of life. For what would you exchange love, joy, peace, patience, kindness, goodness, faithfulness, gentleness, and self-control? Would you rather have a new car, a cabin in the hills, a promotion at work, a motorboat, a jug of wine, or a prostitute? Tragically, many believe such things will bring them love, joy, peace, and so on, but they won't. These positives are the fruit of the Spirit, which is the result of abiding in Christ. There is nothing inherently wrong with a new car, a promotion at work, or a vacation cabin, but their pleasures don't last, and they cannot produce what only our new life in Christ can.

You are sacrificing the temporal to gain the eternal. Some sacrifice! If we truly grasped what was to be gained, we would pursue God and His holiness above all else. The apostle Paul wrote, "Discipline yourself for the purpose of godliness; for bodily discipline is only of little profit, but godliness is profitable for all things, since it holds promise for the present life and also for the life to come" (1 Timothy 4:7-8 NASB). Paul doesn't say that taking care of our natural bodies for the few years we are present on this earth has no value. Bodily discipline does have value, but it is small compared to what can be gained by living a godly life.

Paul is implying that if you shoot for this world, you will miss the next. If you shoot for the next world, though you will not only reap eternal rewards, you will also enjoy the benefits of living a righteous life in this world. Not only will your life be characterized by the fruit of the Spirit, but you will be free to be all that God created you to be. (This is an achievable goal.) Your life will have purpose and meaning. Empowered by His presence, you will fulfill your calling and bear much fruit.

Are you satisfied with your life right now? You can be! Jesus said, "Blessed are those who hunger and thirst for righteousness, for they shall be satisfied" (Matthew 5:6 NASB). Do you believe that? If you did believe that, then what would you be doing? We believe it, because we don't think anything else has any lasting satisfaction.

Why Aren't We Growing?

Other than a lack of proper motivation, why aren't many believers living a righteous life? The prophet Hosea offered one explanation: "My people are destroyed from lack of knowledge" (4:6). Some have never been taught the truth that would set them free nor learned how to live a liberated life in Christ.

Others have learned enough truth in order to experience salvation, but they have never repented or known how to repent. Faith without repentance leads to stagnation with little evidence that salvation ever took place. This further leads to a joyless life, with little motivation to continue on. Suppose a pastor gives a stirring message and challenges people to repent, and many respond. What do they do? Some may confess their sin, which is the first step to repentance—but it is not repentance. Consequently, those who have never fully repented will get caught in the sin-confess-sin-confess-and-sin-again cycle. Eventually most will give up and settle for a mediocre Christian life—or they will fall away, reasoning that the Christian life just doesn't work for them or isn't worth the effort.

Both of us have taught in seminary. We have told our students that the greatest asset they will have in their churches is mature saints, but the greatest liability they will have is saints who got old but didn't mature. All they want to do is censure. *You can't do that around here, young man. We've never done it that way before!* Some actually regress and become *more* critical, arrogant, and judgmental. As believers, we should be *progressing*: able to say, "I am more loving, more peaceful, more patient, (and so on) than I was last year, and I am falling more in love with God and others every day." If we can't say that, then we are not growing, and we are missing out on life.

Paul wrote, "I gave you milk to drink, not solid food; for you were not yet able to receive it. Indeed, even now you are not yet able, for you are still fleshly. For since there is jealousy and strife among you, are you not fleshly, and are you not walking like mere men?" (1 Corinthians 3:2-3 NASB). There are many Christians sitting in our churches who are *unable* to receive God's word. Logically, there must be some way to resolve the jealousy and strife, or there will be no growth.

It has been our privilege to help people all over the world resolve their personal and spiritual conflicts and find out who they are and how they are free in Christ. Until that happens there has been little or no growth in their lives, but once they have experienced their freedom through genuine repentance and faith in God, watch them grow! The Word comes alive to them and they devour it.

There Is Nothing More Rewarding

Paul made it clear: "All Scripture is inspired by God and profitable for teaching, for reproof, for correction, for *training in righteousness;* so that the man of God may be adequate, equipped for every *good work*" (2 Timothy 3:16-17 NASB). The Word is being taught in our Christian schools and churches, and people are being trained to hone their skills for church programs, but how many are receiving the reproof and correction that is needed for training in righteousness? Without such training, we have leaders and followers in the church who are knowledgeable and skillful, but not necessarily righteous. There will be no "good work" without "training in righteousness." There will be a lot of *work*—but not the kind that changes lives and bears fruit for eternity.

This is an immense problem in the church. As seminary professors, we have seen many students become more knowledgeable, but not necessarily more godly. Paul taught that "the goal of our instruction is love from a pure heart and a good conscience and a sincere faith" (1 Timothy 1:5 NASB). God is love, which defines His nature, and becoming like Him should be the purpose of Christian teaching, whether in our seminaries, Bible schools, or churches. If any Christian is going to have an ounce of lasting significance, the proper order is character before career, and maturity before ministry.

Sanctification has to do with attaining that character and maturity. It is the *only* route to a meaningful life as a Christian, as we indicated above. Though it is a word that has frightened many believers, sanctification simply means the process of becoming like our loving God. It means getting closer to Him while moving away from anything that gets in the way of the growth of our relationship with Him.

In this book we are going to explain the essentials of sanctification and how we can grow in Christ.* If we can help you understand this crucial doctrine and be set on a path that is personally fulfilling and rewarding, we will be thrilled. If you are properly motivated to continue on this path, then know that *nothing* can keep you from being the person God created you to be…and that is God's will for your life. The truth will set you

---

* For the Bible student who wants to go deeper into this topic, a much fuller treatment of sanctification is found in our book *God's Power at Work in You* (Harvest House Publishers, 2001).

free, and there is nothing more rewarding than living a liberated life in Christ.

We challenge you to rise above the average and follow the example of Paul, who tells us of his desire and passion: "I count all things to be loss in view of the surpassing value of knowing Christ Jesus my Lord, for whom I have suffered the loss of all things, and count them but rubbish so that I may gain Christ, and may be found in Him...having...the righteousness which comes from God on the basis of faith" (Philippians 3:8-9 NASB).

—Neil and Robert

CHAPTER ONE

The Gospel of Liberation

Freedom ranks after life itself as the quintessence of the human experience. Freedom defines the man; it stamps the divine image upon him.

AUTHOR UNKNOWN

SLAVERY IN THE UNITED STATES WAS ABOLISHED by the Thirteenth Amendment on December 18, 1865. How many slaves were there in the U.S. on December 19? In reality, none, but many still lived like slaves. They did so because they never learned the truth. Others knew and even believed they were free, but chose to continue living as they had always been taught.

Many plantation owners were devastated by the proclamation. "We're ruined! Slavery has been abolished. We've lost the battle to keep our slaves."

But their chief spokesman slyly responded, "Not necessarily. As long as these people think they're still slaves, this proclamation of emancipation will have no practical effect. You don't have a legal right over them anymore, but many of them don't know it. Keep your slaves from learning the truth, and your control over them will not even be challenged."

"But what if the news spreads?"

"Don't panic. We have another barrel on our gun. We may not be able to keep them from hearing the news, but we can still keep them from understanding it. They don't call me the 'father of lies' for nothing. We still have the potential to deceive the whole world. Just tell them that they misunderstood the Thirteenth Amendment. Tell them they are *going* to be free, not that they are free already. The truth they heard is just *positional* truth, not *actual* truth. Someday they may receive the benefits, but not now."

"But they'll expect me to say that. They won't believe me."

"Then pick out a few persuasive ones who are convinced they're still slaves and let them do the talking for you. Remember, most of these newly freed people were born as slaves and have lived like slaves all their lives. All we have to do is deceive them so they still think like slaves. As long as they continue to do what slaves do, it won't be hard to convince them they must still *be* slaves. They'll maintain their slave identity because of the things they do. The moment they try to profess that they're no longer slaves, just whisper in their ear, 'How can you even think you're no longer a slave when you are still doing the things slaves do?' After all, we have the capacity to accuse the brethren day and night."

Years later, many slaves have still not heard the wonderful news that they have been freed, so naturally they continue to live the way they've always lived. Some slaves have heard the good news, but they evaluate it by what they are presently doing and feeling. They reason, *I'm still living in bondage, doing the same things I have always done. My experience tells me I must not be free. I'm feeling the same way I was before the proclamation, so it must not be true. After all, your feelings always tell the truth.* So they continue to live according to how they feel, not wanting to be hypocrites!

One former slave, however, hears the good news and receives it with great joy. He checks out the validity of the proclamation and finds out that the highest of all authorities originated the decree. Not only that, but it personally cost that authority a tremendous price, which he willingly paid so the slave could be free. As a result, the slave's life is transformed. He correctly reasons that it would be hypocritical to believe his feelings and not the truth. Determined to live by what he knows to be true, his experiences begin to change rather dramatically. He realizes that his old master has no authority over him and does not need to be obeyed. He gladly serves the one who set him free.[1]

THE GOSPEL IS THE "PROCLAMATION OF EMANCIPATION" for every sinner who is sold into the slavery of sin. We come into this world born dead in our trespasses and sins (Ephesians 2:1), by nature children of wrath (verse 3). The good news is that Christians are no longer slaves to sin. We are alive in Christ and dead to sin (Romans 6:11). We have been set free in Him. We are forgiven, justified, redeemed, and born-again children of God. But how many Christians are living liberated lives in Christ, and how many understand what it means to be a child of God?

When we were slaves to sin, we could not free ourselves. Likewise, as Christians we can never do for ourselves what Christ has already done for us. Not understanding what He has already accomplished has resulted in many believers desperately trying to become somebody they already are. On the other hand, some people are claiming a perfection that has not yet been realized. If we want to mature in our relationship with God, then we need to understand the difference between what Christ has already accomplished for us and what still needs to be done. We also need to know what part He plays in our sanctification, and what part we play.

Understanding the Good News

The idea of freedom is part of the meaning of *salvation* in the Old Testament. The primary term in it for *salvation*—Hebrew, *yasa*—means "to be roomy or broad...Since this (the making spacious for the one constricted) takes place through the saving intervention of a third party in favor of the oppressed and in opposition to his oppressor, we get the sense 'to come to the rescue' and 'to experience rescue.'"[2]

The idea of salvation in the New Testament carries over the meaning of deliverance and freedom. Paul said, "It is for freedom that Christ has set us free. Stand firm, then, and do not let yourselves be burdened again by a yoke of slavery" (Galatians 5:1). In other words, don't put yourself back under the law as a means by which you relate to God, because you have been set free in Christ.

The root Greek word for salvation—*sozo*—communicates the notion of wholeness, soundness, and health. Salvation is not just getting rid of sin. Rather, salvation frees us from all the hindrances that prevent us from being all we were created to be. Salvation, in its broadest sense, includes deliverance from all that hinders fallen humanity from becoming complete in Christ according to God's design in creating us.

A Futile Existence

In the Fall, what Adam and Eve lost as a result of their sin was *life*. They died spiritually—that is, they lost their relationship with God and became slaves to sin. Every person since that time has been born physically alive but spiritually dead. (Physical death was also a consequence of Adam and Eve's sin, but not for hundreds of years in their case.)

Having no relationship with God, Adam and Eve began a hopeless search for significance. They, as have all their descendants, tried to understand the purpose and meaning of life in their natural state of existence. Natural people are left to wonder, *Who are we, and why are we here?* In their attempts at self-verification they have, "exchanged the truth of God for a lie, and worshiped and served created things rather than the Creator" (Roman 1:25). Lacking a divine perspective, people have "found" their identity and purpose for living in their physical appearance, performance, social status, and the various roles they play.

Trying to make sense of life independently of God is futile, and nobody epitomized that more than Solomon. He appeared to have it all—power, position, status, wealth, and sex (he had 1000 wives and concubines). He owned the plantation! He had everything that people lust after, but something was missing. Like any natural man, he sought to find purpose and meaning in life independently of God. Not only did Solomon have the ultimate opportunity to pursue the meaning of life, but he also had more God-given wisdom than any other mortal to interpret his own findings. In the book of Ecclesiastes he registered his conclusion: "'Meaningless! Meaningless!' says the Teacher. 'Utterly meaningless! Everything is meaningless'" (1:2).

Antidote: The Whole Gospel

The reason many believers still struggle with their own identity and purpose for living is because they have not understood the whole gospel. They have probably heard that Jesus is the Messiah who died for their sins. If they receive Him into their hearts, God will forgive them of their sins, and they will get to go to heaven when they die.

There are three things that are wrong or incomplete with that kind of gospel presentation. First, it gives the impression that eternal life is something we get when we die. That is not true—but no wonder it leaves Christians thinking they're forgiven sinners instead of redeemed saints. No—every child of God has eternal life the moment he or she is born again. "He who has the Son has life; he who does not have the Son of God does not have life" (1 John 5:12).

Second, if you were going to save dead people, what would you do? Cure the condition they died of? If that is all you did, they would still be dead. To save the dead, you would have to perform two functions: First, of course, you have to cure the disease that caused them to die. The Bible teaches that the "wages of sin is death" (Romans 6:23). So Jesus went to the cross and died for our sins—but that is not the whole gospel. Second, you would have to *give them life.* The second half of the verse reads, "The gift of God is eternal life in Christ Jesus our Lord" (Romans 6:23b). What Jesus came to give us was spiritual—that is, eternal—life which means that you are a child of God and your soul is in union with Him.

Third, "the reason the Son of God appeared was to destroy the devil's work" (1 John 3:8). Satan had deceived Eve, and Adam sinned. Consequently the first couple lost their relationship with God, and Satan became the rebel holder of earthly authority. Jesus affirmed this when He referred to Satan as the "prince of this world" (John 14:30). Because of what Christ accomplished, "the prince of this world now stands condemned" (16:11). Jesus "has rescued us from the domain of darkness and brought us into the kingdom of the Son he loves, in whom we have redemption, the forgiveness of sins" (Colossians 1:13-14).

Jesus said, "I have come that they may have life, and have it to the full" (John 10:10). He was not talking about our present physical life, which people try to make full by an abundance of earthly pleasures and possessions. He was talking about our spiritual life, which is our relationship with God. Fullness of life is exemplified in the fruit of the Spirit, which is "love, joy, peace, patience, kindness, goodness, faithfulness, gentleness, and self-control" (Galatians 5:22-23). Jesus was talking about a redeemed human community that is fully alive in Christ.

The Meaning of Sanctification

Our making this new life in Christ real in our experience is related to our becoming like Him, separated from sin. In Scripture, life is always related to righteousness. As physical life is robbed by toxic foreign substances in our body, so spiritual life is sapped by the presence of sin. Thus, in order that we might experience His life, God commands us to "be holy, because I am holy" (1 Peter 1:16; Leviticus 11:44-45; 19:2; 20:7; see also Matthew 5:48).

Sanctification refers to our being made like God in His holiness. The Old Testament Hebrew word for *holy* and the corresponding Greek term in the New Testament have the basic meaning of *being set apart to God or the realm of the sacred as distinct from all other things*. These same terms stand behind the English words *sanctify*, *sanctification*, and *saint*. Because the realm of God is separate from sin, *sanctification* thus speaks of that aspect of our salvation in which we are separated *to* God's holiness and *away from* sin.

Salvation Is Past, Present, and Future

The concepts of salvation and sanctification can be a little confusing unless you understand that both are presented in Scripture as past, present, and future. The verb tenses used reflect this. In other words, the Bible says we *have been* saved, we *are presently being* saved, and we *will someday be fully* saved. Notice the past tenses in the following verses declaring that "in Christ" we "have been saved":

> Because of his great love for us, God, who is rich in mercy, made us alive with Christ even when we were dead in transgressions—it is by grace you *have been saved*...It is by grace you *have been saved*, through faith—and this is not from yourselves, it is the gift of God (Ephesians 2:4-5,8).

> Join with me in suffering for the gospel, by the power of God, who *has saved* us and called us to a holy life—not because of anything we have done but because of his own purpose and grace (2 Timothy 1:8-9).

> When the kindness and love of God our Savior
> appeared, *he saved us,* not because of righteous
> things we had done, but because of his mercy. He
> saved us through the washing of rebirth and
> renewal by the Holy Spirit (Titus 3:4-5).

These passages clearly teach that every child of God has
experienced salvation. We have been born again; consequently,
we are now spiritually alive. Jesus said, "I am the resurrection
and the life. He who believes in me will live, even though he
dies; and whoever lives and believes in me will never die" (John
11:25). In other words, we will continue to live spiritually when
we physically die.

Scripture also teaches that we are *presently* "being saved,"
according to the following passages:

> The message of the cross is foolishness to those who
> are perishing, but to us who are *being saved* it is the
> power of God (1 Corinthians 1:18).

> We are to God the aroma of Christ among those
> who are *being saved* and those who are perishing
> (2 Corinthians 2:15).

> My dear friends, as you have always obeyed—not
> only in my presence, but now much more in my
> absence—continue to work out your salvation with
> fear and trembling (Philippians 2:12).

We do not *work for* our salvation, but we have a responsibility to *work out* what God has born in us. As we will see later,
there is also a progressive aspect of sanctification, which is similar in concept to the continuing process of salvation. That is, we
are "being saved," and we *are* presently being conformed to the
image of God. Theologian Charles Hodge makes clear this connection between sanctification and salvation:

> Salvation principally consists in…transformation of the heart. Jesus is a Savior because He saves His people from their sins…
>
> A state of salvation is a state of holiness. The two things are inseparable because salvation is not mere redemption from the penalty of sin, but deliverance from its power. It is freedom from bondage to the appetites of the body and the evil passions of the heart; it is an introduction into the favor and fellowship of God, the restoration of the divine image to the soul, so that it loves God and delights in His service. Salvation, therefore, is always begun on earth.[3]

Salvation begins on earth, but it is completed in heaven. That is why Scripture speaks about a *future* aspect of salvation. The following passages teach that we "shall be saved":

> Since we have now been justified by his blood, how much more *shall* we *be saved* from God's wrath (Romans 5:9-10).

> The hour has come for you to wake up from your slumber, because *our salvation is nearer* now than when we first believed (Romans 13:11).

We have not yet realized our salvation from the "coming wrath" (1 Thessalonians 1:10), but we have the assurance that when that wrath comes, we will be saved from it.

> Having believed, you were marked in him with a seal, the promised Holy Spirit, who is a deposit guaranteeing our inheritance until the redemption of those who are God's possession—to the praise of his glory (Ephesians 1:13-14).

Just like salvation, the biblical concept of sanctification begins at our new birth in Christ and ends in the final perfection of glorification. Scripture speaks of the believer's sanctification as already accomplished, as being accomplished, and as finally being completed in the future. These are often referred to as the three tenses of sanctification. In the next chapter, we are going to identify and explain these three tenses, and then we'll devote the rest of the book to looking at how we as Christians conform to the image of God.

QUESTIONS FOR THOUGHT AND DISCUSSION

1. How did the slavery metaphor speak to you?

2. After the Fall, what is the spiritual condition of all those who come into this world through natural birth? (See Ephesians 2:1.)

3. What would be your perception of yourself, and how would it affect the way you live, if all Christ had done was to die for your sins?

4. What did Adam and Eve lose in the Fall, and what did Christ come to give us? What does that mean to you?

5. What does it mean that Christ came to undo the works of Satan, and how does that affect you?

6. Explain the whole gospel.

7. Are Christians already sanctified, or are they being sanctified?

CHAPTER TWO

The Beauty of Holiness

*The beauty of holiness has done more, and will do
more, to regenerate the world and bring in everlasting
righteousness than all the other agencies put together.*

THOMAS CHALMERS

EVERY LIVING ORGANISM MOVES through the three progressive
stages of birth, growth, and maturation. Each stage has its own
contribution, characteristics, scope, and limits as to what it can
supply to the overall purpose of the organism. For example, who
or what the organism will be is established at conception. From
that stage on, no creature or plant can be anything other than
what the Creator intended it to be if it is going to fulfill its purpose. The growth stage cannot alter what the organism is; it can
only ensure that the organism reaches its greatest potential.

Our new birth as Christians is a critical part of our salvation
as well as our sanctification. We were both identified and set
apart as new creatures in Christ from the moment we were
born again. As Christians we are not trying to *become* children
of God—we *are* children of God who are becoming like
Christ. We are admonished to put off childish things and grow
in our relationship with God. We are presently growing in
sanctification—with each stage of growth building upon the
previous one—until the time of our final glorification.

As we consider this growth process, just as we need to understand the three stages of salvation, we also need to understand the three tenses of sanctification—past, present, and future. God has made us holy, continues to make us holy, and ultimately assures us of perfect holiness.

Past-Tense Sanctification

The past tense is often called *positional* sanctification because it speaks of the holy position, or status, that the believer has "in Christ." The *positional* truth of who we are in Christ is real truth—not just a useful fiction—and it is the basis for the *progressive* (present-tense) sanctification that follows. Just as the past-tense *reality* of salvation is the basis for the present-tense *working out* of our salvation, so also is our *position* in Christ the basis for our *growth* in Christ. At salvation the believer is set apart, or separated, to God and thus participates in God's holiness. Notice how Peter shows this cause and effect:

> His divine power *has granted* [past tense] to us everything pertaining to life and godliness, through the true knowledge of Him who called us by His own glory and excellence. For by these He *has granted* [past tense] to us His precious and magnificent promises, so that by them you may become partakers of the divine nature, *having escaped* [past tense] the corruption that is in the world by lust (2 Peter 1:3-4 NASB).

For many believers, *sanctification* has become synonymous with *growth* or *maturity*, thus putting emphasis on the present-tense use of the word. In Scripture, however, the words *sanctification*, *sanctify*, *saints*, and *holy* are most often used in the past tense. For example, in the opening of his letter to the Corinthian believers, Paul addresses them as "those sanctified in Christ Jesus" (1 Corinthians 1:2). Describing the change that took place at salvation, he says to them, "You were washed, you were sanctified, you were justified in the name of the Lord Jesus Christ and by the Spirit of our God" (1 Corinthians 6:11).

Even though he identifies Christians as saints, Paul wrote sternly to the believers at Corinth because they had many problems. So when Paul said the Corinthians were sanctified, he did not mean that they were living righteously or that they were mature in their character. Rather, they were holy because they were alive "in Christ."

When we receive Christ we are given "an inheritance among all those who are sanctified" (Acts 20:32). Jesus said to Paul, "I am sending you to them [the Gentiles] to open their eyes and turn them from darkness to light, and from the power of Satan to God, so that they may receive forgiveness of sins and a place among those who are sanctified by faith in me" (Acts 26:17-18). According to both of these passages, by our faith in Christ we belong to the company of believers, who are described as *already* sanctified.

The status of those who have been sanctified is prominent in the book of Hebrews, where Christ is portrayed as the great High Priest, who is superior to the old priesthood of the Levites. Holiness—past-tense sanctification—is central to Christ's priesthood in Hebrews. "We *have been made* holy [past tense] through the sacrifice of the body of Jesus Christ once for all" (Hebrews 10:10; see also 10:29 and 13:12).

Sinner or Saint?

The New Testament describes believers as "saints," which means "holy ones" (Romans 1:7; 2 Corinthians 1:1; Philippians 1:1). Being a saint does not necessarily reflect a person's present measure of growth in character, but it does identify those who are rightly related to God. In the King James Version of the Bible, believers are called "saints," "holy ones," or "righteous ones" more than 200 times. In contrast, unbelievers are called "sinners" more than 300 times. Clearly, the term "saint" is used in

Scripture to refer to the believer, and "sinner" is used in reference to the unbeliever.

Paul's reference. Although the New Testament gives us plenty of evidence that a believer is capable of sinning, it never unequivocally identifies the believer as a sinner. Often mentioned as an exception is Paul's reference to himself in which he declares, "I am foremost" of sinners (1 Timothy 1:15 NASB). However, despite Paul's use of the present tense, the description of himself as the foremost of sinners is a reference to his preconversion opposition to the gospel. Taking this as a truthful statement, we can conclude that he indeed was the chief of all sinners, because nobody opposed the work of God with more zeal than Paul, in spite of the fact that he could boast, "As for legalistic righteousness, [I am] faultless" (Philippians 3:6). There are several reasons why we believe 1 Timothy 1:15 refers to what Paul was before he came to Christ.

First, Paul's reference to himself as a sinner is in support of the first part of his declaration: "Christ Jesus came into the world to save sinners." The reference to "the ungodly and sinners" in verse 9 of 1 Timothy 1 (NASB), along with the other New Testament uses of the term *sinners*,[4] shows that the "sinners" whom Christ came to save are individuals *outside of salvation* rather than believers who can still choose to sin.

Second, Paul's reference to himself as a sinner is immediately followed by the words, "Yet...I *found* [past tense] mercy" (verse 16 NASB), clearly pointing to the past occasion of his conversion. Paul was still astonished by the mercy God had extended to him, who was the worst of sinners. Paul makes a similar evaluation of himself based upon the past when he says, "I *am* [present tense] the least of the apostles and do not even deserve to be called an apostle, because I persecuted the church of God" (1 Corinthians 15:9). Because of his past actions, Paul considered himself unworthy of what God's grace and mercy had made him: an apostle that was "not in the least inferior to the most eminent apostles" (2 Corinthians 11:4 NASB; see also 12:11).

Third, although Paul declares that he is the worst sinner, a few verses earlier he also declares that Christ had strengthened him for the ministry, having considered him "faithful"—or trustworthy—for the service to which he was called (1 Timothy 1:12). The term "sinner" in verse 15, then, does not describe Paul in his state of being a believer, but rather is being used in remembrance of what he was before Christ took hold of him.

James' reference. The only other places in Scripture that are sometimes taken as referring to Christians as sinners are both in the book of James. The first, "Wash your hands, you sinners" (James 4:8), is one of ten action commands urging anyone who reads this general epistle (a letter written to the church everywhere in the world) to make a decisive break with the old life. We believe this is best understood as calling the reader to repentance and therefore salvation. The second use of "sinner" (James 5:20) appears to be a reference to unbelievers as well. The "sinner" is to be turned from the error of his ways and thus be saved from "death." Since this verse is referring to *spiritual* death, it suggests that the person was not a believer. In both instances, James was using the term *sinner* as it was used in particular among the Jews to speak of those "who disregarded the law of God and flouted standards of morality."[5]

The fact that these sinners are among the people addressed by James does not necessarily mean that they are believers, for Scripture teaches that unbelievers can reside in the presence of saints (see 1 John 2:19), as they surely are doing today in our churches. James' reference to them as sinners fits the usual New Testament description of those who have not come to repentance and faith in God, since the rest of Scripture clearly identifies believers as saints who still have the capacity to sin.

Confrontation with the righteousness of God frequently brought deep acknowledgment of a person's present sinful condition. Peter's recognition of himself before the Lord as a "sinful man" is not uncommon among the saints (Luke 5:8). Though believers can be sinful, Scripture does not identify them as sinners.

God's choice. The status of being "saints" is parallel to the concept of being God's "called" or "elect" ones. Believers are those who are "loved by God...called to be saints" (Romans 1:7, that is, they are saints by virtue of being called). They are "God's chosen [or elected] people, holy and dearly loved" (Colossians 3:12). They are "chosen...through sanctification by the Spirit" (2 Thessalonians 2:13; 1 Peter 1:2 NASB). God chose and separated them out from the world to be His people. Believers are "holy brothers" (Hebrews 3:1).

By the "election" and "calling" of God, believers are set apart to Him and belong to the sphere of His holiness. Even though we begin our walk with God as immature babes in Christ, we are children of God. As "saints" set apart into God's holy realm, we are now to grow in our likeness to Him. That is, we are to grow in practical holiness of life through the resources that are ours in Christ. Paul combined these two concepts of holiness when he wrote to the Ephesians. Addressing them as "saints" or "holy ones" in chapter 1, verse 1, he goes on in verse 4 to say that God "chose us in him [Christ]...to be holy and blameless in his sight." God's choosing or electing of these believers in Christ made them "holy ones" for the ultimate goal of growing to be conformed to His holiness in their character.

Made Holy Through Christ

Our positional holiness is based on the fact that we are new creations in Christ. Believing faith joins us to Christ so that we now share in all that Christ is, including His holiness. As Paul says, "By His [God's] doing you are in Christ Jesus, who became to us wisdom from God, and righteousness and sanctification, and redemption" (1 Corinthians 1:30 NASB).

Past-tense sanctification means that believers have been brought into fellowship with a holy God. Scripture says that only those who are clean and holy can enter His presence to worship and have fellowship with Him. As sinners we could not enter His holy presence. But by faith in Christ, who sacrificed

Himself to cleanse us of our sins, we are joined to Him and have been invited into the very "holy of holies" of heaven to have fellowship with God. Christ's sacrifice for our sins means that God no longer holds the uncleanness of our sins against us. He now welcomes us into His holy presence because we are clothed in Christ's holiness.

What About Sin?

As believers we still have the capacity to sin, and we do so when we fail to believe the truth and walk according to the flesh. Such poor choices, however, do not disbar us from God's presence: "The death he [Christ] died, he died to sin once for all" (Romans 6:10). That means that our past, present, and future sins are already forgiven. When Christ died "once for all," how many of your sins were future? They all were! Hebrews 10:14 tells us that "by one sacrifice he [Christ] has made perfect forever those who are being made holy." Despite the fact that we do sin, God says that "we have confidence to enter the Most Holy Place by the blood of Jesus…and since we have a great priest over the house of God, let us draw near to God with a sincere heart in full assurance of faith, having our hearts sprinkled to cleanse us" (verses 19,21-22).

Past-tense sanctification does not mean that we do not sin or have no sin. "If we claim to be without sin, we deceive ourselves and the truth is not in us" (1 John 1:8). But "having" sin as a believer "in Christ," and "being" basically sinful in nature, are two different issues. To say that Christians are depraved like they were prior to salvation is like the plantation owner telling his slaves they really aren't free, but they will be someday.

It is counterproductive to identify Christians as "sinners" saved by grace and then expect them to act as saints. Telling people who they are in Christ does not give them a license to sin. Rather, being alive in Christ is the only means by which they can *stop* sinning. That is one reason why "the Spirit himself testifies with our spirit that we are God's children" (Romans 8:16).

This is critical to understand for the sake of our growth—because nobody can consistently behave in a way that is inconsistent with what they believe about themselves. We *were* sinners in desperate need of God's grace, but "now we *are* children of God, and what we will be has not yet been made known. But we know that when he appears, we shall be like him, for we shall see him as he is. Everyone who has this hope in him purifies himself, just as he is pure" (1 John 3:2-3).

If believers are still fundamentally sinners by nature, then shouldn't sin be their dominant pattern of life? Isn't that what sinners do? What do saints do, though? According to John, those who understand they are children of God and have their hope fixed on Jesus purify themselves. They live according to who they really are—children of God.

Present-Tense Sanctification

God performed a gracious work when He called us out of darkness into His marvelous light and granted us the status of holiness by virtue of our union with Christ. He did this so that He could carry on His work of making us holy. The process of growing from carnality into the likeness of Christ is commonly called *progressive* sanctification, or *experiential* sanctification. Paul describes this: "Now that you have been set free from sin and have become slaves to God, the benefit you reap leads to holiness [or sanctification], and the result is eternal life" (Romans 6:22).

Progressive sanctification is the present focus of God's work in our lives. We can define it as God working in the lives of His children, setting them free from sin's bondage and progressively renewing them into the image of His own holiness in attitude, character, and actions of life. The Westminster Catechism defines sanctification as "the work of God's free grace whereby we are renewed in the whole man after the image of God and are enabled more and more to die unto sin and live unto righteousness."

In justification, God declares the believer righteous because of the righteousness of Christ, which is accounted to the believer.

Justification is the act of a judge. It removes from the sinner the condemnation that is deserved because of the *guilt* of sin. In other words, we are forgiven. Sanctification, however, is more the act of a priest, and deals with the *pollution* of sin. The Reformed theologian Louis Berkhof explained sanctification as "that gracious and continuous operation of the Holy Spirit, by which He delivers the justified sinner from the pollution of sin, renews his whole nature in the image of God, and enables him to perform good works."[6]

Justification and sanctification are distinct concepts—the former more related to the guilt of sin, and the latter to its pollution—but they are vitally related. When we are joined to Christ through faith, we are clothed in His righteousness and thereby stand justified before God. In Christ's righteousness we stand in a right relationship to God in relation to His righteous law. But we are also accepted into God's presence as clean and pure in Christ's holiness. At the same moment we were justified, we were sanctified positionally. The Spirit of God came into our lives and began the process of transforming our character through progressive sanctification, or Christian growth.

Progressive sanctification is a challenge to believers. "Having these promises, beloved, let us cleanse ourselves from all defilement of flesh and spirit, perfecting holiness in the fear of God" (2 Corinthians 7:1 NASB). We are urged to sexual purity because "it is God's will that you should be sanctified" (1 Thessalonians 4:3). Elsewhere we are told, "Make every effort to live in peace with all men and to be holy; without holiness no one will see the Lord" (Hebrews 12:14).

Conforming to God's Image

Although the Bible speaks of past-tense sanctification more frequently than present-tense sanctification, the concept of progressively being made holy is a dominant theme of Scripture. Terms like *growth, edification, building up, transformation, purification, renewing* all relate to the process of being conformed to the image of God. In Colossians 2:6-7 Paul reveals the process in a nutshell: "As you have received Christ Jesus the Lord, so walk in Him, having been firmly rooted and now being built up in Him and established in your faith, just as you were instructed, and overflowing with gratitude" (NASB).

In past-tense sanctification we were "rooted in Christ," and it is only from this foundation of union with Christ that we can be built up. Paul wrote to the church in Corinth, "I have sent to you Timothy, who is my beloved and faithful child in the Lord, and he will remind you of my ways which are *in Christ,* just as I teach everywhere in every church" (1 Corinthians 4:17 NASB). Terms like "in Christ," "in Him," or "in the Beloved" are among the most repeated phrases in the epistles. They confirm that we are new creations in Christ and that our souls are in union with God: that is, we are spiritually and eternally alive in Christ.

John uses the metaphors of little children, young men, and fathers to describe the process of Christian growth (1 John 2:12-14). Little children are those who have entered into a knowledge of God and have had their sins forgiven. They have overcome the *penalty* of sin. Fathers, who are more mature, have had a long-term understanding and knowledge of God. Young men know the Word of God, are strong, and are characterized as those who have overcome the evil one. In other words, they have overcome the *power* of sin.

How are we going to help fellow believers mature in the faith if they don't know who they are in Christ and don't know how to overcome the evil one? In all the years that we have been helping people find their identity and freedom in Christ we have found one common denominator among all defeated Christians. They don't know who they are in Christ, nor do they understand what it means to be a child of God. They are ignorant of their spiritual heritage. They are like the slaves who had heard the news that they were free, but were still held hostage by the plantation owner with his double-barreled shotgun.

A Key Clarification

Paul affirmed both past- and present-tense sanctification in the same epistle. In Colossians 1:28 he wrote, "We proclaim Him, admonishing every man and teaching every man with all wisdom, so that we may present every man complete in Christ" (NASB). Later he declared, "In Him [Christ] you have been made complete, and He is the head over all rule and authority" (2:10 NASB). This seems like a contradiction. In the first verse, Paul was admonishing the Colossians to be complete in Christ, and in the second verse he said they were already complete in Christ. How do we reconcile these two verses? In 1:28 the word "complete" means *mature* or *perfect*, and refers to the process of present-tense sanctification that will be fully realized only with future final sanctification. Paul used a different Greek word for "complete" in Colossians 2:10, a word that means *to fill*. The apostle's point is that "in Christ" we are complete—we have everything that pertains to *salvation*. That passage refers to past-tense salvation and sanctification.

Scripture clearly presents both the past-tense and present-tense aspects of sanctification. We will confuse ourselves in our walk with God if we emphasize one truth at the expense of the other. One extreme is to say that our sanctification has already been fully completed. Therefore, there is no need for any activity on our part to become like Christ. Such an extreme view has led some to believe that they haven't sinned since they became Christians. They have failed to see the present-tense teaching of sanctification. At the other extreme are people who do not understand who they are in Christ. They don't comprehend what has already happened at salvation, nor do they understand positional sanctification. Such people end up trying to become somebody they already are. We cannot do for ourselves, however, what Christ has already done for us. We are already complete in Christ—and the continuing work of salvation is to "present every man complete [mature] in Christ" (Colossians 1:28 NASB).

The New Man: Becoming Fully Human

We are so accustomed to sin and imperfection as character-istics of our humanity that we think to be human is to be flawed. But such is not the case. Becoming holy is not simply about being conformed to the likeness of God, it is also about being made fully human. J.I. Packer wrote that godliness or holiness "is simply human life lived as the Creator intended—in other words, it is perfect and ideal humanness, and existence in which the elements of the human person are completely united in a totally God-honoring and nature-fulfilling way."[7] There is great joy in becoming holy, because we're entering into the *fullness* of our humanity! Holiness is not about conforming to the rules of an authoritarian rule-maker. Rather, "it is about the celebration of our humanity."[8]

Future-Tense Sanctification

The future tense of sanctification is expressed in Paul's explanation of the work and goal of Christ's sacrifice for us: "Christ loved the church and gave himself up for her to make her holy, cleansing her by the washing with water through the word...to present her to himself as a radiant church, without stain or wrinkle or any other blemish, but holy and blameless" (Ephesians 5:25-27). Paul, in his prayers for other believers, frequently mentioned this ultimate aim. His desire was for the ultimate perfection of believers:

> May the Lord make your love increase and overflow for each other and for everyone else, just as ours does for you. May he strengthen your hearts so that you will be blameless and holy in the presence of our God and Father when our Lord Jesus comes with all his holy ones (1 Thessalonians 3:12-13— note love's central place in sanctification).

May God himself, the God of peace, sanctify you through and through. May your whole spirit, soul and body be kept blameless at the coming of our Lord Jesus Christ. The one who calls you is faithful and he will do it (1 Thessalonians 5:23-24).

QUESTIONS FOR THOUGHT
AND DISCUSSION

1. In what way are you already sanctified?

2. As a believer, are you a sinner, or are you a saint—and what impact does that have on your perception of yourself and how you live?

3. If Scripture identifies believers as saints, then how do we explain Paul's reference to himself as the chief of all sinners?

4. On what basis are we positionally sanctified at conversion?

5. Explain the difference between justification and sanctification.

6. What defines the three stages of growth explained by John?

7. Read Ephesians 1:1-17 and count the number of times Paul says we are "in Christ" or "in Him." Obviously we have a rich inheritance, but the problem is we don't always seem to comprehend it. Why do you think Paul then prayed as he did in Ephesians 1:18-19?

CHAPTER THREE

A Right Standing Before God

Vice is a monster of so frightful mien,
As to be hated needs but to be seen;
Yet seen too oft, familiar with her face;
We first endure, then pity, then embrace.

ALEXANDER POPE*

ADAM'S SIN RESULTED IN THE SEPARATION of humanity from a holy God. Even to this day there are two orientations human beings have toward sin, which are diametrically opposite of each other. Both are debilitating. The first orientation is that of people who seem to have no moral conscience or any awareness of their own sin. The prophet wrote, "Were they ashamed because of the abomination they have done? They were not even ashamed at all; they did not even know how to blush" (Jeremiah 6:15 NASB). They obviously have no relationship with God.

The other debilitating orientation toward sin is held by those who have a relationship with God. They are justified (forgiven) in the eyes of God, but they are overwhelmed by their sins and cannot seem to accept God's forgiveness. They try to

*During Pope's time (1688–1744), the term *vice* was commonly used as a synonym for *sin*.

39

earn God's favor and are often trapped in the bondage of legalism. They are plagued with condemning thoughts by the accuser of the brethren (Revelation 12:10), and question their own salvation. They may intellectually know that "there is now no condemnation for those who are in Christ Jesus" (Romans 8:1), but they can't seem to rest in that truth. The following personal story sent to Neil by a missionary reveals this struggle:

> Though I have been a Christian for many years, I never understood God's forgiveness and my spiritual inheritance. I have been struggling for years with a particular sin. I was in Bible college when I began this horrible practice. I never thought this living hell would ever end. I would have killed myself had I not thought that was a sin. I felt God had turned His back on me and I was doomed to hell because I couldn't overcome this sin. I hated myself. I felt like such a failure.
>
> The Lord led me to purchase your book *Victory Over the Darkness*. I now feel like a new Christian, like I've just been born again. My eyes are now open to God's love, and I realize that I am a saint who has chosen to sin. I can finally say I am free—free of Satan's bondage, and aware of the lies he has been feeding me.
>
> Before, I would confess to God and beg His forgiveness when I sinned, but the next time I would fall deeper into Satan's grasp because I couldn't accept God's forgiveness and couldn't forgive myself. I always thought the answer was to draw closer to God, but I went to Him in confusion, believing I was a sinner who couldn't be loved. *No more!* Through the Scriptures and the way you presented them to me, I am no longer a defeated Christian. I now know I am alive in Christ, dead to sin, and a slave of righteousness. I now live by faith according to what God said is true. Sin has no power over me; Satan has lost his grip on me.

The True Nature of Sin

Growth in the Christian life is dependent upon God's grace-giving presence in our lives; therefore, to grow, we must be rightly related to Him. Before we receive Christ, sin separates us from the righteous and holy God. Our natural state is described by the apostle Paul as being born dead (spiritually) in our trespasses and sins (Ephesians 2:1). Consequently we are "separated from the life of God" (4:18). Before we can grow we must have a relationship with God. This requires dealing with the reality of sin.

Scripture declares that all people are naturally sinners: "All have sinned and fall short of the glory of God" (Romans 3:23). All are "under sin" as an alien power that dominates their life and brings guilt and condemnation before God as well as self (Romans 3:9; Galatians 3:22). Horatius Bonar, in his study of God's way of holiness, noted that "he who would know holiness must understand sin."[9]

It is difficult for us to grasp the true nature of sin for several reasons. First, we have always been personally involved in sin and lived in an environment conditioned by sin. We cannot fully grasp the difference between living in sin and living in righteousness because we have never experienced perfect righteousness.

Second, our understanding is skewed because of our own sinfulness. People tend to think less of their sin than they should in order to excuse themselves. Rather than confess wrongdoing, we often rationalize: *Well, everybody does it!* Or, *I'm not as bad as that guy over there.* Such comparisons are merely relative—as opposed to comparing ourselves to God, who is sinless. Our righteous deeds are like filthy rags (Isaiah 64:6) when compared to God's righteousness.

Third, our natural awareness of what is sinful can easily grow dull with tolerance and exposure to sin. For example, the profanity and explicit sex commonly accepted in today's television and movies would never have been tolerated 50 years ago.

Fourth, we haven't experienced the full weight of sin's consequences. If we got at this moment what we deserved, we would immediately be cast into hell. If people knew the damage caused by the sins they think they've gotten away with, they would cover their faces in shame. Secret sin on earth is open scandal in heaven. Despite God's occasional judgments upon sinful people throughout history, the full consequences of sin have not yet been poured out on anyone.

To better understand the true nature of sin, we must look at the cross of Christ. There, the power of sin was unleashed from hell through sinful men, in the utmost hatred, in an attempt to kill the most righteous and loving person to ever walk on the face of the earth. The cross also demonstrates the power of sin and its full consequences, which are spiritual death—separation from God.

Scripture not only shows the heinousness of sin, but also reveals it as a power superior over all human effort. It "reigns" as king over fallen humanity resulting in death (Romans 5:21). Sin is not mere ignorance that can be overcome by education. Sin is more than bad habits that can be overcome by the practice of moral disciplines. It is more than a twisted personality that can be overcome by secular psychology. Sin is a power that enslaves us. Paul's cry represents the reality of all people under sin's domination: "What a wretched man I am! Who will rescue me from this body of death? Thanks be to God—through Jesus Christ our Lord!" (Romans 7:24-25). Only the superior power of God in Christ can redeem fallen humanity from the reigning power of sin.

A Relationship Broken by Sin

Adam and Eve were created to have a relationship with God, which is the *true* "natural" state of humanity—living in fellowship with God. Satan's temptation (as is every temptation) was an attempt to get Adam and Eve to exercise their will independently of God. They disobeyed God by eating the forbidden fruit of the "tree of the knowledge of good and evil." The real essence of sin is seen in Satan's words, "Your eyes will be opened, and you will be like God, knowing good and evil" (Genesis 3:5).

To have knowledge of good and evil means to have such full knowledge that one is now the determiner of what is good and evil. Thus when Adam and Eve chose to eat of the forbidden tree, they were saying, *We reject God as the One who determines what is right or wrong. We will determine for ourselves what is good for us, and we think that eating this fruit is, in fact, for our good.* They assumed for themselves the prerogative to determine what is right or wrong. They played right into the hands of the devil, who is a deceiver and the father of lies.

Satan had mixed some distorted truth with his lie. Adam and Eve "acted" like gods in determining for themselves what was right. But what they determined *wasn't* right—and rather than embracing the truth that would preserve their freedom, they believed a lie that led to death and bondage to sin. Sin is the inevitable consequence of rebellion toward God; "everything that does not come from faith is sin" (Romans 14:23). Sin is the "unbendable bent of every person who does not possess life from God."[10]

Since God is the only source of life, living apart from God can only mean death. Being separated from God, Adam and Eve and all their descendants have had to find their own means to survive. Acting like gods, fallen humans struggle to gain acceptance, security, and significance through physical appearance, performance, and status. Any threat to their security becomes a source of anxiety or anger. Every manifestation of sin, from negative attitudes to hurtful actions, stems from the one root of all sin—namely, the desire to act as god over their own lives.

A Break in Our Legal Relationship

There is another aspect in which our fellowship with God has been broken by sin. He has established a moral order for the harmonious relationship of all created beings. Fellowship with Him and others is experienced by living according to the laws. Sin is the breaking of His righteous laws, which brings a break in fellowship, and also our "legal relationship" with Him.

The sinner stands under God's condemnation as a lawbreaker: "Cursed is everyone who does not continue to do everything written in the Book of the Law" (Galatians 3:10). Although Paul's statement has specific reference to the Old Testament Law of Moses, it applies to all people in relation to God's moral laws. All people are said in the Bible to be "shut up," "imprisoned," or "under sin," which means that they are under the power and condemnation of sin (verse 22).

Sin not only brings God's condemnation, but also pollution and corruption into the life of the sinner. It makes what is pure and holy become defiled and impure. The moral nature of a sinner is in opposition to God's moral nature. We cannot have fellowship with God unless we are pure and clean, for "what fellowship can light have with darkness?" (2 Corinthians 6:14).

In summary, sin has broken humanity's legal relationship with God, causing us to stand guilty and under the condemnation of God. Sin has also broken our personal moral relationship with Him, causing our nature to be impure and at odds with God's holiness and purity.

Restoring the Legal Relationship

Suppose an employee whom you personally chose to manage your estate decides to rebel against you and leave. This happens because your most formidable competitor has been feeding him a pack of lies and wooing him over to his side. As a result, the relationship you had cultivated and nourished for the employee's own good is broken. Your competitor then subjects your former employee to a subservient existence in a coal mine, which eventually leads to his contracting black lung and dying. Would you be willing to do what is necessary to help save such a person?

How many of us would be? The natural person would likely respond or at least think, *That self-seeking traitor got what he deserved. Let him die in the coal mine.* How many of us would be willing to take the initiative to win him back at the cost of sacrificing the life of their only son?

No illustration can come close to capturing the incredible love that God demonstrates when He takes the initiative to restore a person's relationship with Himself—especially when the fault lies entirely with the sin of the person. "God so loved the world that he gave his one and only Son, that whoever believes in him shall not perish but have eternal life" (John 3:16). It was *God* who sought Adam and Eve in the Garden of Eden after they sinned.

Our legal relationship with God is restored through *justification.* Justification is a judge's pronouncement of a person's right standing before the law. Justification is the *declaration of righteousness* rather than the *making of one righteous*, which is made clear when it is used as the opposite of *condemnation* (Romans 8:33-34). When a judge condemns someone, he does not *make* the person a sinner, he simply *declares* that such is the case. In pronouncing us justified, God is not *making* us inherently righteous, He is *declaring* that we are in right standing before His law.

Justification is God's declaration of our righteousness, or right standing before Him as the moral Lawgiver of the universe. The condemnation due our sins has been removed. This change of legal relationship is purely a gift from Him, which is made clear in Romans 3:21-26:

> Now a righteousness from God, apart from law, has been made known, to which the Law and the Prophets testify. This righteousness from God comes through faith in Jesus Christ to all who believe. There is no difference, for all have sinned and fall short of the glory of God, and are justified freely by his grace through the redemption that came by Christ Jesus. God presented him as a sacrifice of atonement,

through faith in his blood. He did this to demonstrate his justice, because in his forbearance he had left the sins committed beforehand unpunished—he did it to demonstrate his justice at the present time, so as to be just and the one who justifies those who have faith in Jesus.

Several truths in this passage are critical to note. First, the righteousness that provides the basis on which God can declare us right is *His* and not ours. It is a "righteousness from God, apart from law," or apart from our keeping His law. We are not saved by how we behave, but rather by what we believe.

Second, the righteousness made available to us is the righteousness that is *in Christ*. Our justification is "through the redemption that came by Christ Jesus." He satisfied God's wrath and judgment against us as breakers of His moral law. "Christ redeemed us from the curse of the law by becoming a curse for us" (Galatians 3:13).

This is a point that needs some expansion. For God to declare us righteous, more is necessary than just the forgiveness of our sins. Christ took the consequences of our sins upon Himself, providing forgiveness that erases the penalty of sin; but the positive righteousness by which God can declare us righteous is made possible by Christ's total obedience to God. "Through the obedience of the one man the many will be made righteous," as Paul explained in Romans 5:19.[11]

Because of God's declaration, we are alive "in Christ Jesus, who has become for us wisdom from God—that is, our righteousness, holiness and redemption" (1 Corinthians 1:30). Christ is "our righteousness" because we are "in Him." We are "clothed...with garments of salvation and arrayed...in a robe of righteousness" (Isaiah 61:10). This aspect of our justification comes through the imputing of Christ's righteousness to us so that "in Him" we stand righteous before God.

Third, our justification is totally a matter of God's grace. We are "justified freely [as a gift] by his grace" (Romans 3:23). Finally, our justification comes to us solely through faith in Jesus Christ. "This righteousness from God comes through faith in Jesus Christ to all who believe." God justifies those who have "faith in Jesus" (verse 22; see also verses 26,30). Forgiveness of sins and a positive righteousness in Christ are God's gracious gift to which we can add nothing...and nothing more is needed. All that is "required" of us is to receive the free gift of eternal life, gratefully accept God's forgiveness, and believe that we are fully justified before God by virtue of the blood of the Lord Jesus Christ.

Peace with God

"Since we have been justified through faith, we have peace with God through our Lord Jesus Christ" (Romans 5:1). Many Christians, though, live under a false condemnation as if they are walking on eggshells, hoping that God won't find out what they've done or what they're really like. When they make some mistake they think, *I'm going to get it now!* They have a fearful anticipation that the hammer of God is going to fall upon them.

Dear Christian, the hammer has already fallen. It fell on Christ. We *have been* justified [past tense], and we *have* peace with God *right now*. There is now no condemnation for those who are in Christ Jesus (Romans 8:1). Although there is a place for possessing a proper fear of God's chastisement if we persist in sin, the greatest motivation to live a holy life should not be the threat of impending doom. Rather, we are motivated to draw near to Him out of love—love born out of gratitude for what He has done for us. Let me (Neil) illustrate.

The school district in the farming community where I was raised used to have a program called religious day instruction. Classes were shortened on Tuesday afternoons so students could go to the church of their choice. Those who didn't want to go to church went to study hall. One Tuesday afternoon, a friend of mine and I skipped religious day instruction and played in the city gravel pit. The next day the principal called me in and confronted me with the fact that I had skipped school. He concluded his remarks by saying that he had arranged for me to be home from school on Thursday and Friday of that week. I was in shock, thinking that I had been suspended from school for two days because I had skipped religious day instruction.

I was terrified as I rode the bus home from school that afternoon. I was not looking forward to seeing my parents. I slowly walked down our long lane, fearing the prospect of having to face the wrath of Mom and Dad. I thought about faking an illness for two days...or maybe I could get dressed as though I were going to school, but instead hide in the woods until it was time to come home! No, I couldn't do that to my parents. Lying wasn't the answer.

There was no peace in my heart as I trudged up that lane. There was no way I could hide from my parents what I had done. When I told my mother, she was at first surprised—then she started to smile. *Oh, Neil, I forgot to tell you I called the principal earlier this week and asked permission for you to be released from school for two days to help us pick corn.*[12]

Incredible! Had I known that staying home Thursday and Friday was already justified, would I have feared facing my parents? Would the ride home have been an agonizing experience? If I had known the truth, I would have raced up that lane and joyfully looked forward to seeing my mom and dad!

Dear Christian, we are not sinners in the hands of an angry God. We are saints in the hands of a loving God. If we truly grasped the truth that we have been justified, we would go running to our heavenly Father. "We may approach God with freedom and confidence" (Ephesians 3:12). Therefore, "let us draw near to God with a sincere heart in full assurance of faith, having our hearts sprinkled to cleanse us from a guilty conscience" (Hebrews 10:22).

Access to God

Being fully justified also brings the privilege of access into God's presence. Under the old covenant only the Levitical high priest—on the basis of animal sacrifice—had access into the presence of God in the Holy of Holies. Now, because of Christ's sacrifice, all believers are welcome into God's holy presence.

Paul describes this as an access "into this grace in which we now stand" (Romans 5:2). We are unconditionally loved and accepted by God because of who He is and because of what Christ has already accomplished for us. "Let us then approach the throne of grace with confidence, so that we may receive mercy and find grace to help us in our time of need" (Hebrews 4:16).

Restoring Our Personal Moral Relationship

Sin also caused a break in humanity's personal *moral relationship* with God. He is holy and pure, and only those who are likewise can enjoy fellowship and intimacy with Him. Because the natural person is sinful by nature, a change is required. As we have seen earlier, believers are sanctified, or holy, in Christ. This is often called *positional sanctification*. It is not based on a person's own holiness, but rather on the holiness of Christ, to whom they have been joined through faith.

But this *positional* sanctification must not be understood in a way that denies a real, *personal* change in relation to our holiness. When we were set apart to the realm of God's holiness in Christ, we were also separated from the authority and power of sin, which reigns in the realm of sin in which we formerly existed. Thus Paul tells us to consider ourselves alive in Christ and dead to sin (Romans 6:11). Considering it doesn't *make* it so—we are to consider it so because it *is* so. Because we are alive in Christ, sin no longer has any rightful authority over us. We belong to a new master; we have been freed from the bondage of sin.

For this reason some have preferred to use the term *definitive*, rather than *positional*, to describe this foundational, past-tense aspect of sanctification.[13] It means, in a word, that we are new creations in Christ. We are no longer "in Adam"—we are "in Christ." We can say with Paul, "I have been crucified with

Christ and I no longer live, but Christ lives in me. The life I live in the body, I live by faith in the Son of God, who loved me and gave himself for me" (Galatians 2:20). Definitive sanctification, which takes place at the point of our salvation in Christ, is the indispensable point from which we now grow in progressive, or experiential, sanctification.

This is not pie-in-the-sky theology or wishful thinking. Every child of God *has been reconciled* to God. Being new creations in Christ is the core issue, apart from which there can be no further growth. Consider these words from Paul:

> You are all sons of God through faith in Christ Jesus, for all of you who were baptized into Christ have clothed yourselves with Christ. There is neither Jew nor Greek, slave nor free, male nor female, for you are all one in Christ Jesus. If you belong to Christ, then you are Abraham's seed, and heirs according to the promise...Because you are sons, God sent the Spirit of his Son into our hearts, the Spirit who calls out, "Abba, Father." So you are no longer a slave, but a son; and since you are a son, God has made you also an heir (Galatians 3:26-29; 4:6-7).

Recognizing Our New Identity

Peace and acceptance with God are what makes it possible for us to experience *practical* sanctification (which is another way to term experiential sanctification). True spiritual growth happens only when we have a personal relationship with God. We are no longer at enmity with God. We can now enjoy a relationship in which we are conformed more and more into His likeness.

As we have indicated before, growth will not take place if we still see ourselves as slaves of sin and live under the fear of condemnation. Only as we see ourselves as children of God can we really grow in holiness (see Romans 8:15). When we are free from the task of trying to gain a relationship to God by our own righteousness, then we are free to appropriate His righteousness for our growth.

The disciples were challenged to bear fruit (John 15:16) because they were *already* attached to the vine. They were to grow from a position of "cleanness" ("you are already clean"— 15:3). They did not have to work to become clean.

Finally, Paul says that we are "transformed in his [Christ's] likeness" as our faces are turned toward the Lord and we reflect His glory (2 Corinthians 3:18). We turn our faces toward Him as friends, ones who are no longer alienated. As Bonar put it, "Reconciliation is indispensable to resemblance; personal friendship must begin a holy life."[14] Through Christ, we are His friends: "I no longer call you servants, because a servant does not know his master's business. Instead, I have called you friends" (John 15:15).

As children of God we have the assurance that God will supply all our needs "according to His riches in glory in Christ Jesus" (Philippians 4:19 NASB). The most critical needs, which are wonderfully met in Christ, are the "being" needs. They are life itself, identity, acceptance, security, and significance. Read through the list of scriptures below, which was taken from Neil's book *Who I Am in Christ*.[15]

In Christ...

...I am accepted:

John 1:12	I am God's child
John 15:15	I am Christ's friend
Romans 5:1	I have been justified
1 Corinthians 6:17	I am united with the Lord and am one with Him in spirit
1 Corinthians 6:20	I have been bought with a price—I belong to God

1 Corinthians 12:27	I am a member of Christ's body
Ephesians 1:1	I am a saint
Ephesians 1:5	I have been adopted as God's child
Ephesians 2:18	I have direct access to God through the Holy Spirit
Colossians 1:14	I have been redeemed and forgiven of all my sins
Colossians 2:10	I am complete in Christ

...I am secure:

Romans 8:1-2	I am free from condemnation
Romans 8:28	I am assured that all things work together for good
Romans 8:31-34	I am free from any condemning charges against me
Romans 8:35-39	I cannot be separated from the love of God
2 Corinthians 1:21-22	I have been established, anointed, and sealed by God
Philippians 1:6	I am confident that the good work that God has begun in me will be perfected
Philippians 3:20	I am a citizen of heaven
Colossians 3:3	I am hidden with Christ in God
2 Timothy 1:7	I have not been given a spirit of fear, but of power, love, and a sound mind
Hebrews 4:16	I can find grace and mercy in time of need
1 John 5:18	I am born of God and the evil one cannot touch me

...I am significant:

Matthew 5:13	I am the salt and light of the earth
John 15:1,5	I am a branch of the true vine, a channel of His life
John 15:16	I have been chosen and appointed to bear fruit
Acts 1:8	I am a personal witness of Christ
1 Corinthians 3:16	I am God's temple
2 Corinthians 5:17-20	I am a minister of reconciliation
2 Corinthians 6:1	I am God's co-worker
Ephesians 2:6	I am seated with Christ in the heavenly realms
Ephesians 2:10	I am God's workmanship
Ephesians 3:12	I may approach God with freedom and confidence
Philippians 4:13	I can do all things through Christ who strengthens me

QUESTIONS FOR THOUGHT
AND DISCUSSION

1. Why would someone approach God in a sinful state if they thought He was a vindictive judge?

2. Can you relate to the missionary's personal story? How?

3. Why can't we fully understand the problem of sin?

4. How would you define sin?

5. What does justification bring us?

6. Are Christians just forgiven, or has there been a moral change in our nature?

7. How does being a new creation in Christ meet our greatest needs?

CHAPTER FOUR

A New Heart

Holiness means something more than
the sweeping away of the old leaves of sin:
it means the life of Jesus developed in us.

I. LILIAS TROTTER

EVERY FARMER UNDERSTANDS cause and effect. If you don't feed the sheep, they die. If you don't sow seeds in the spring, there will be nothing to harvest in the fall. I (Neil) lived on a farm in Minnesota, and after I finished eighth grade, my family moved to Arizona. I remember how excited I was to see palm and citrus trees. In those days, fresh fruit was not readily available in most places, so the idea of picking an orange from a tree right in our own backyard was exciting to me. What I didn't know was that we had an ornamental orange tree, which was pretty to look at—but the fruit was not fit to eat. Ornamental oranges are a hardy stock, so the city used them in parks and along boulevards because they could survive the frost.

Ornamental orange trees are also used for root stock. They grow in a nursery to a certain height; then the trunk is severed above the ground, and a new life (such as a navel orange) is grafted in. Everything below the graft retains the characteristics of the ornamental orange.

The orange-tree picture illustrates how many believers think of themselves. By forgiving their sins in Christ, God has cut off a lot of the obvious manifestations of the old life and replaced them with characteristics of Christ, they believe. But at the root, where others can't see, they're still the same old sinner.

There is one major problem with this kind of thinking. It is a lie. It does not agree with what Scripture says is true of us. For instance, the apostle Paul never identifies believers according to their inheritance in Adam. Why? Because they no longer are in Adam! Paul recognizes them for who they are in Christ, and admonishes us to do the same. "From now on we recognize no one according to the flesh" (2 Corinthians 5:16 NASB).

Though we as branches retain the outward appearance of our old source (Adam), every believer has been grafted into Christ, who is the source of our new life. As in nature, unless there is some seed or root giving life to an organism, no growth can take place. Spiritual growth apart from Christ is impossible. Shoots that bear no fruit can grow out from us, but they must be cut off. We must crucify the outgrowth of the old life.

The New Birth

We have noted before that Adam and Eve were born both physically and spiritually alive. Because of sin, they died spiritually. They were separated from God. Consequently their descendents are born into this world physically alive but spiritually dead (Ephesians 2:1). Like an ornamental orange tree, they may look good, but their fruit is bitter. It drops to the ground and brings forth more natural stock that will look good only for a season.

The basic human makeup comprises an outer person (a material body) and an inner person (an immaterial soul or spirit). Created in the image of God, we have the capacity to think, feel, and choose. The center of the person is the heart— the "wellspring of life," according to Proverbs 4:23—and in our natural state, "the heart is deceitful above all things and beyond cure" (Jeremiah 17:9). It has also been conditioned, from the time of our natural birth, by the deceitfulness of a fallen world rather than by the truth of God's Word. Although no two-dimensional diagram is adequate to show who we are, the following is a functional depiction of the natural person:

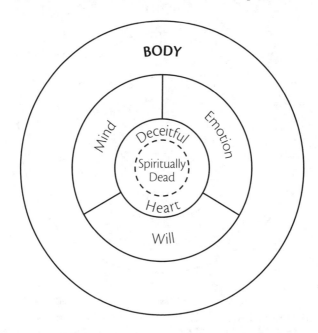

Ezekiel prophesied God's answer for the natural human condition: "I will give you a new heart and put a new spirit in you; I will remove from you your heart of stone and give you a heart of flesh" (36:26). Under the covenant of grace God says, "I will put my laws in their hearts" (Hebrews 10:16). Jesus came that we might have life, and the believer receives spiritual life and a new identity at the moment of salvation: "To all who received him, to those who believed in his name, he gave the right to become children of God" (John 1:12).

The moment you were grafted into Jesus, the true vine, you were sanctified, or set apart as a child of God. "You are already clean" (John 15:3), and you will continue to be sanctified as He prunes you so that you may grow and bear fruit. The following diagram depicts every born-again child of God:

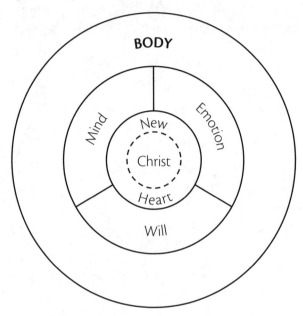

God has given us a "new birth into a living hope through the resurrection of Jesus Christ from the dead," as the apostle Peter puts it (1 Peter 1:3). We have been "born again...through the living and enduring word of God" (1:23). Peter calls new Christians "newborn babies" and challenges us to "crave pure spiritual milk, so that by it you may grow up" (2:2).

Jesus said, "I tell you the truth, no one can enter the kingdom of God unless he is born [again]...you must be born again" (John 3:5,7). The Greek term refers to both being born *again* and *born from above*.[16] It is a birth from heaven by the Spirit (verse 8). This new birth is also described as *regeneration*, which has the idea of a new beginning. As Paul teaches us, we have been saved "by the washing of regeneration" (Titus 3:5 NASB).

Our Identification with Christ

Every believer has been united with Christ in His death and resurrection:

> Don't you know that all of us who were baptized into Christ Jesus were baptized into his death? We were therefore buried with him through baptism into death in order that, just as Christ was raised from the dead…we too may live a new life (Romans 6:3-4).

Paul testified of this reality, "I have been crucified with Christ and I no longer live, but Christ lives in me. The life I live in the body, I live by faith in the Son of God, who loved me and gave himself for me" (Galatians 2:20). The apostle was saying, "I died, but I live, obviously a new and different person" (see also Colossians 3:1-3). In accord with this, Paul identifies every believer with *Christ:*

• in His death	Romans 6:3,6; Galatians 2:20; Colossians 3:1-3
• in His burial	Romans 6:4
• in His resurrection	Romans 6:5,8,11
• in His ascension	Ephesians 2:6
• in His life	Romans 6:10-11
• in His power	Ephesians 1:19-20
• in His inheritance	Romans 8:16-17; Ephesians 1:11-12

A New Creation

Paul wanted every new believer to know that "if anyone is in Christ, he is a new creation; the old has gone, the new has come!" (2 Corinthians 5:17)—and that he is part of God's restoration plan for all creation. The phrase, "he is a new creation," could be translated as "there is a new creation." Paul was teaching that through Christ's death and resurrection, a new creation has been effected, in which *all* things—all of creation, the earth and the heavens—will finally be made new (Revelation 21:1; see also Isaiah 65:17; 66:22; 2 Peter 3:13). The believer who has died and now lives in Christ is part—and a first fruit—of this new creation.

The believer has put on "the new self" (Colossians 3:9-10). The "new self"—which is literally the "new man"—refers both to the corporate new humanity "in Christ," and the new person and identity of the individual as a part of that new creation. Bible scholar F.F. Bruce says, "The new man who is created is the new personality that each believer becomes when he is reborn as a member of the new creation whose source of life is Christ."[17]

The fact that we are a new creation in Christ may seem confusing to us, because we still have the same physical appearance—and many of the same old thoughts and feelings. Because so much appears to remain unchanged after we become Christians, it is tempting to think that our newness refers only to our position in Christ—a position that will not be realized until we get to heaven. That has led some to believe that there is no *real* change in us until we are finally glorified. However, that would be like teaching justification without regeneration (we are forgiven, but there is no new life). If we are still ornamental orange trees after salvation, then how can we hope to bear navel oranges? In order to grow we *have* to believe that our new identity is rooted in the life of Christ—and that is why a primary work of the Holy Spirit is to bear witness with our spirit that we are children of God (Romans 8:16).

Experiencing the New Creation

We "know that our old self was crucified with Him" (Romans 6:5). As we have already noted, the phrase "old self" is literally "old man." The "old man" in relation to the believer has been crucified in Christ, and he has put on the "new man" (Colossians 3:10)—the "new self, created to be like God in righteousness and holiness" (Ephesians 4:24). Notice that, "Our old self *was crucified*" (past tense). Some try and try to put the old man to death and they can't do it. Why not? Because he is already dead. If we don't understand this truth we are likely to wonder, *What has to happen in order for me to experience the life of the new man—the new creation?* The only thing that has to happen *already* happened nearly 2000 years ago, and the only way we can enter into that experience is by faith. We cannot do for ourselves what Christ has already done for us.

An older saint told me (Neil), "I have struggled for 22 years in ministry and I finally think I know what the answer is. I came across the following passage: 'You died, and your life is now hidden with Christ in God' (Colossians 3:3). That's it, isn't it?" I assured him that it was. Then he asked, "How do I do that?" I suggested that he read the passage just a little bit more slowly. For 22 years this dear man had been desperately trying to *become* somebody he already is—and many other believers have been doing likewise. What we *do* does not determine who we *are*. Who we are and what we believe about ourselves determines what we do. We don't labor in the vineyard hoping that God may someday love us. God already loves us, and that is why we labor in the vineyard. We don't serve God with the hope that someday He will accept us. We already are accepted in the Beloved—that is why we serve Him.

Under the new covenant of grace we are instructed to believe what God says is true, and live accordingly by faith, and then the new life works itself out in our experience. If we try to *make* it true by our experience, we will never get there. Paul points out the futility of such thinking in Galatians 3:2: "I would like to learn just one thing from you: Did you receive the Spirit by observing the law, or by believing what you heard? Are you so foolish? After beginning with the Spirit, are you now trying to attain your goal by human effort?"

We are saved by faith, and we walk or live by faith. We *have been* sanctified by faith, and we *are being* sanctified by faith.

Later, we will see that our activity is involved in the process of our sanctification. But ultimately, we are neither saved nor sanctified by how we behave, but by how we believe. What we do is just a product of what we think and believe.

A New Master, A New Dominion

As mortals, we have no choice but to live under a spiritual power: either our heavenly Father, or the god of this world, Satan (2 Corinthians 4:4). When we become a new creation in Christ, there is a change of dominion over our lives. The "old man," referring to the old humanity in Adam, and the "new man," referring to the new humanity in Christ, are spheres of existence that are determined by events and the powers associated with them. The old man is determined by the sin of Adam and is therefore dominated by the power of sin. The new man is determined by the righteous obedience of Christ and is ruled by the power of his new resurrection life.

Dying to the old sphere means dying to the powers that dominated it and coming into a new life under a new power. In brief, God has "rescued us from the dominion of darkness and brought us into the kingdom of the Son he loves" (Colossians 1:13). Bible commentator Peter O'Brien observes,

> Like a mighty king who was able to remove peoples from their ancestral homes and to transplant them…into another realm, God had taken the Colossians (Christians) from the tyranny of darkness…where evil powers rule (Luke 22:53) and where Satan's authority is exercised (Acts 26:18), transferring them to the kingdom in which His beloved Son held sway.[18]

Before we became new creations in Christ, we were slaves to sin (Romans 6:16-17; 7:23,25—the "law of sin"), or to "impurity and to ever-increasing wickedness" (6:19). We had no choice because "sin reigned in death" (5:21), and thus death reigned over us (5:14,17). The change of dominion over our lives as believers is described by Paul in Romans 6:6-7. Our old self—that is, our unregenerate self as individuals existing in the old natural sphere of sinfulness—was crucified with Christ and our slavery to sin and death has come to an end through our union with the death and resurrection of Christ. Paul is arguing that what is true about Christ we should count true about ourselves, because we are "in Christ." The goal of our crucifixion with Christ was "so that the body of sin might be done away with, that we should no longer be slaves to sin" (6:6). The "body of sin" refers to the person or self (living in the present bodily form) under the rule of sin. The old self that was in bondage to sin and therefore utilized all of our bodily existence in servitude to sin and its mastery died with Christ. Now a new self exists that is no longer under the taskmaster of sin. This new self can be utilized as an instrument of righteousness in service to God (6:11-13).

Free to Live Abundantly

Because they have died *with Christ* (participated with Him in His death to sin), believers are therefore free from the mastery of sin and can live a liberated life *in Christ,* as expressed by Paul:

> Just as you used to offer the parts of your body in slavery to impurity and to ever-increasing wickedness, so now offer them in slavery to righteousness leading to holiness. When you were slaves to sin, you were free from the control of righteousness... But now that you have been set free from sin and have become slaves to God, the benefit you reap leads to holiness, and the result is eternal life (Romans 6:19,21-22).

Physical death has no mastery over us either. "Now if we died with Christ, we believe that we will also live with him. For we know that since Christ was raised from the dead, he cannot die again; death no longer has mastery over him" (6:8-9).

When we physically die, we will be fully sanctified, receiving a new resurrected body and being ushered into the presence of God. Those who are free from the fear of physical death are free to live in Christ "because through Christ Jesus the law of the Spirit of life set [us] free from the law of sin and death" (Romans 8:2).

Just as the proclamation of the Thirteenth Amendment brought freedom to the slaves in America, so too has the gospel brought freedom to us. Paul says, "Now that you have been set free from sin, and have become slaves to God, the benefit you reap leads to holiness, and the result is eternal life" (Romans 6:22). The god of this world is to us as the plantation owners were to the slaves. The owners still wanted to be served, as does the devil. Neither does he want you to know the freedom you have in Christ. He will try to keep you from the truth that sets you free.

Being under the dominion of God does not eliminate our responsibility to choose. We have the capacity to "present" ourselves to either master (Romans 6:13,19; 12:1). Nevertheless, we cannot escape the mastery of the dominion under which we live—which for the believer is very good news!

A New Person with New Desires

Identifying with Christ in His death and resurrection involves more than an external change of master. It also involves a transformation within ourselves. Our very being is changed at its deepest core. The propensities of our lives—the deepest desires of our hearts—are now oriented toward God rather than toward self and sin. We have a "change of nature."*

At salvation we have been given a new heart (Ezekiel 11:19; 36:26). Our heart is who we really are as persons (Proverbs

---

*We are using the word *nature* in the sense of our prevailing characteristics or dispositions. We are not using the word in the sense of our nature as human beings as compared to, say, the feline nature of cats. As humans, we all have the same human nature, but that nature can have different propensities and forces at work in it. So when we talk about a change in nature, we are referring to a change in the *fundamental* orientation, propensities, desires, or direction of our person, including our thoughts and actions.

27:19; 1 Peter 3:4). A new heart thus makes us a new person; we are "born again." According to Paul, this inner transformation is what defines us: "A man is not a Jew if he is only one outwardly, nor is circumcision merely outward and physical. No, a man is a Jew if he is one inwardly; and circumcision is circumcision of the heart, by the Spirit, not by the written code. Such a man's praise is not from men, but from God" (Romans 2:28-29).

The need for a new heart is the basic message of the Sermon on the Mount. For instance, Jesus said, "I tell you that anyone who looks at a woman lustfully has already committed adultery with her in his heart" (Matthew 5:28). He wasn't saying that a person committed adultery by looking, but that looking lustfully at a woman is the evidence that a person has already committed adultery in his heart. What needs to be changed is the heart. The heart not only reflects who we are, it also directs our life. We live according to the condition of our heart. Proverbs 4:23 exhorts us, "Above all else, guard your heart, for it is the well-spring of life."

The last part of the above verse literally means, "for out of it are the issues of life." The heart is the fountain of life that controls the course of our life. The direction our life takes is determined by the heart, according to Ecclesiastes 10:2: "A wise man's heart *directs him* toward the right, but the foolish man's heart *directs him* toward the left" (NASB).

Jesus taught that what we do comes from our heart: "Out of the overflow of the heart the mouth speaks. The good man brings good things out of the good stored up in him, and the evil man brings evil things out of the evil stored up in him" (Matthew 12:34-35). Our thoughts, motives, words, feelings, attitudes, and actions all originate from our heart. As believers, the control center of our life has been made new.

The Propensity of the Heart

It is the nature of the human heart to be controlled by an outside master. As Robert Jewett puts it, "A characteristic of the heart as the center of man is its inherent openness to outside impulses, its directionality, its propensity to give itself to a master and to live towards some desired goal."[19] This is true because we are not the source of our own life. The heart and soul of humanity was never designed by God to function as master. We are dependent creatures, and therefore by nature we look outside of ourselves for life. Self-seeking, self-serving, self-justifying, self-glorifying, self-centered, and self-confident living is in reality serving the god of this world.

Not only is the heart open to receive from the outside, but as Jewett's statement suggests, what the heart takes in also becomes its master, stamping the heart with its character. Jesus instructed His disciples to store up treasures that could not be destroyed, concluding with the statement, "Where your treasure is, there your heart will be also" (Matthew 6:21). Bible teacher D.A. Carson noted, "The point is that the things most highly treasured occupy the 'heart,' the center of the personality...and thus the most cherished treasure subtly but infallibly controls the whole person's directions and values."[20]

Desiring Change

The Old Testament revealed that the heart of the natural person is deceitful above all things and beyond cure (Jeremiah 17:9). While the heart of the new person still carries remnants of the old, Jeremiah's picture of the heart is not a picture of the new heart of the believer. Those "beyond cure" remnants now stand at the periphery of the real core of the true believer, who is God-oriented and thus bent toward righteousness. Calvin wrote, "God begins His good work in us, therefore, by arousing love and desire and zeal for righteousness in our hearts; or, to speak more correctly, by bending, forming, and directing, our hearts to righteousness."[21]

The disposition of the heart of a true believer is toward God. Although we still sin, this sin is related to a more surface level of our being. The flesh will act contrary to the real person of the heart. Even though we can walk or live according to the flesh, doing so does not change the real nature of our heart nor our identity. In fact, this very issue points to what may be the surest way to determine whether or not a person is a Christian. Christians will have a sense of conviction if they do something contrary to the nature of God. If people sense no remorse or conviction when they sin, they should legitimately question their salvation.

Let the Truth Be Written in Your Mind, Emotions, and Will

The more you affirm who you are in Christ, the more your behavior will reflect your true identity. Commenting on chapter six of Romans, John Stott wrote, "The necessity of remembering who we are [is the way] Paul brings his high theology down to the level of practical everyday experience."[22] Stott continues,

> So, in practice we should constantly be reminding ourselves who we are. We need to learn to talk to ourselves, and ask ourselves questions: "Don't you know? Don't you know the meaning of your conversion and baptism? Don't you know that you have been united to Christ and His death and resurrection? Don't you know you have been enslaved to God and have committed yourself to His obedience? Don't you know these things? Don't you know who you are?" We must go on pressing ourselves with such questions, until we reply to ourselves: "Yes, I do know who I am, a new person in Christ, and by the grace of God I shall live accordingly."[23]

Take the time to meditate on what it means to be a new creation in Christ. Let this truth sink in. It can change your life. The following personal story from one of our former students illustrates this truth. He was one of the most gifted, personable, and intelligent students we have had the privilege of teaching. He attended one of Neil's seminars and later wrote him the following letter:

> I've always figured I was a rotten, no-good, dirty, stinking sinner, saved by grace yet failing God miserably every day. And all I could look forward to was a lifetime of apologizing every night for not being the man I know He wants me to be: "But I'll try harder tomorrow, Lord." As a firstborn, trying so hard to earn the approval of parents with high expectations, I've related to God the same way. *He just couldn't possibly love me as much as He does other, "better" believers. Oh sure, I'm saved by grace through faith, but really I'm just hanging on until He gets tired of putting up with me here and brings me home to finally stop the failure in progress.* Whew, what a treadmill!
>
> When you said, "You're not a sinner, you're a saint," in reference to our new, primary identification, you totally blew me away! Isn't that strange that a guy could go clear through a good seminary and never latch onto the truth that he is, indeed, a new creation in Christ?! I'm convinced that old tapes, laid down in early childhood, can truly hinder our progress in understanding who we are in Christ. Thank you for your clear teaching in this area. It has been so helpful and liberating to me. I'm beginning to grow out of my old negative thoughts about myself and God. I don't constantly picture Him as disappointed in me any more. I have been so deeply touched by what I've learned that I'm taking some people through a study of Ephesians so we can see who we are *in Christ* and what we have as believers *in Christ.* My preaching is different, and our people are profiting greatly, being built up in strength and confidence. Each day of service is a direct gift from God, and I bank each one carefully in heaven's vault for all eternity, to the honor and glory of my Savior!

Questions for Thought and Discussion

1. Apply the illustration of being grafted in to your own identity and growth.

2. Describe your new identity and position in Christ.

3. What is the practical significance of having a new master?

4. Why should you be free from the fear of death?

5. In what way are you free from sin, and does that correspond to your actual experience? Why or why not?

6. Why do we still sin, and how can we stop?

7. What is the heart?

CHAPTER FIVE

Enlarging the Heart

*Holiness is religious principle put into action. It is
faith gone to work. It is love coined into conduct;
devotion helping human suffering, and going up in
intercession to the great source of all good.*

FREDERIC D. HUNTINGTON

IN HIGHER EDUCATION WE HAVE a tendency to focus on
enlarging the minds of our students, but God is trying to enlarge
our hearts. Before Christ, our inner core was shaped by the
world we live in, and our minds were programmed to live independently of God. Sanctification is the process of changing the
heart, which is the center where all elements of personhood
come together in inseparable union.

H. Wheeler Robinson counted 822 uses of the word *heart* for
some aspect of human personality in the Old Testament.
According to his categorization, 204 of the passages related to
the mind, 195 to the will, and 166 to the emotion.[24] It is better to
think of the heart as the center of reflection or contemplation
rather than the seat of our emotions. We stymie sanctification
when we intellectually acknowledge the truth in such a way that
it never touches the heart. Doing so reduces our walk with God
to an intellectual exercise. When there is no personal transformation, "knowledge makes arrogant" (1 Corinthians 8:1 NASB).

When the truth enters the heart, it immediately touches our emotions, which in turn drives the will. Only in the heart do the mind, emotion, and will converge into one harmonious whole. We will discuss in chapter 7 how to renew the mind, but for now consider the following diagram. As God enlarges our hearts, we are being renewed in the inner person in an ever-expanding spiral of growth. We are being transformed by the renewing of our minds, which also includes emotional maturity and a greater sense of self-control as we exercise our wills in agreement with God.

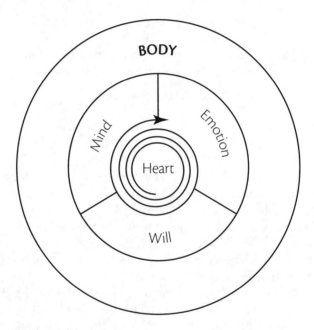

To illustrate, suppose you are riding with a friend in your car after church. A CD is playing inspirational Christian music. Your ears are receiving the sound, but you are tuning it out as you carry on a conversation with your friend. There is a lull in the conversation, and you mentally "tune in" to the music and find yourself caught up in it. Tears start rolling down your cheeks, and you can't help but express yourself. You find yourself singing along, wanting to share what that music is doing to you. You just allowed the music to enter your heart and it affected you mentally, emotionally, and volitionally.

Being alive and free in Christ is a relational experience. We are connected to God, but we can tune Him out. It is very easy to read, hear, and even discuss His Word without appropriating it into our hearts. For instance, there are those who will sit in judgment of the message on Sunday morning instead of letting the message sit in judgment of them: "The Word of God is living and active and sharper than any two-edged sword, and piercing as far as the division of soul and spirit...and able to judge the thoughts and intentions of the heart" (Hebrews 4:12 NASB).

Having taught worship at a seminary, I (Neil) found myself critiquing worship services when I was invited to speak in churches, until one day I realized what I was doing. Nobody at the service needed to worship God that morning more than I did. I needed to acknowledge His presence and experience it. The congregation needed to hear from God, not me, and I needed to know that what I was sharing was coming from Him.

The Cycle of the Expanding Heart

We are being renewed in the inner person as the truth penetrates our hearts. As the heart expands, it is taking back the ground in our souls that was conditioned by this world. Our mind is being renewed, our damaged emotions healed and released, and our will directed in a way that is pleasing to God. Christian growth is like a Slinky that is being stretched to its limits. We cycle from one experience to another as we ascend upward and outward in Christian maturity. Paul shows this cycle of growth in Colossians 1:9-12. (The fact that you can even begin to grow is based on the truth that God "has qualified you to share in the inheritance of the saints in the kingdom of light"—verse 12.) The apostle shares how we can grow by giving us the foundational elements, which are included in the following diagram:

The Cycle of Growth

The growth process begins with a knowledge of God's will, which is found in His Word. His truth must enter our hearts in order for us to spiritually understand how it applies to life in all wisdom. The cycle isn't complete, however, until we choose to live according to what we understand. Living by faith requires us to exercise our will by being submissive through humble obedience. When we do, we grow in the knowledge of God, and the cycle comes full circle, back to where we started. In other words, we will receive greater knowledge as we act out the knowledge we already have. The spin-offs of this growth cycle are increasing spiritual strength, endurance, patience, joy, and thankfulness, all of which become increasingly evident in our character.

The cycle can be blocked at any one of the four points in the diagram. As already described, we can block it at the first stage by reading the Bible as an academic exercise and never seeking to apply it to our lives. We will have knowledge, but not necessarily wisdom and understanding. We can be *increasing in knowledge*, but we won't be *growing* unless the truth enters our hearts. Such knowledge understands the Bible only from a human perspective. Wisdom is seeing life and ourselves from God's perspective.

At stage two, God's Word can penetrate our hearts and consequently convict us of sin and give us discernment and direction for life. But the growth process will again be stymied if we never actually repent, act on our discernment, or step out in faith. The usual hindrance here is fear, such as fear of failure or fear of rejection. Fear of anything other than God is mutually exclusive of faith in God. We are to encourage one another to step out in faith, "for God did not give us a spirit of timidity, but a spirit of power, of love and of self-discipline" (2 Timothy 1:7).

At the third stage, we grow and bear fruit when we decide to live by faith. We actually gain knowledge from our experiences. Our faith can have only one object and that is God (and His Word), but maturity gained through living causes us to understand the Word of God in a way that we didn't before. If we fail to live by faith, however, we won't bear any fruit.

Finally, we can stop the process of growth at stage four by failing to come back to the Word of God. The danger of successfully bearing fruit or experiencing victory is that we can decide to rest on our laurels and think we have arrived. Paul's encouragement in Philippians 3:12-14 is helpful here, as he speaks of his desire to know Christ and everything that goes along with it:

> Not that I have already obtained all this, or have already been made perfect, but I press on to take hold of that for which Christ Jesus took hold of me. Brothers, I do not consider myself yet to have taken hold of it. But one thing I do: Forgetting what is behind and straining toward what is ahead, I press on toward the goal to win the prize for which God has called me heavenward in Christ Jesus.

The Experience of Becoming Who We Already Are

This cycle of growth is dependent upon who we already are. We have pointed out previously the crucial truth that, as believers, we are not trying to become children of God. We are children of God who are becoming like Christ. That is why it is important to understand our position in Christ. Positional sanctification is the basis for progressive sanctification. The epistles always have a tension between what has already been done and what is continuing to take place in our sanctification.

We have learned from Romans 6:6 that our old self was crucified with Christ when we were united with Him in His death by faith. This was a decisive and definite act in the believer's past. Paul exhorts believers to stop living in the old sins of their past life "since you have taken off your old self [man] with its practices and have put on the new self [man]" (Colossians 3:9-10). Growth in holiness takes place when we claim the reality of these past events and act on them.

That is Paul's point in Ephesians 4:22-24:

> You were taught, with regard to your former way of life, to put off your old self, which is being corrupted by its deceitful desires; to be new in the attitude of your minds; and to put on the new self, created to be like God in true righteousness and holiness.[25]

Bible commentator Andrew Lincoln explains that this passage is challenging believers to make the acts of the past a reality in the present:

> Putting off the old person has already taken place through baptism which transferred believers to the new order. This injunction is not an exhortation to believers to repeat that event but to continue to live out its significance by giving up on that old person that they no longer are. *They are new people who must become in practice what God has already made them, and that involves the resolve to put off the old way of life as it attempts to impinge*. This is made clear by the qualifying phrase which precedes the mention of the old person—"as regards your former way of life."[26]

We must renew our minds to the truth that a change *has* taken place in us and then live accordingly by faith, with the confidence that it will work out in our experience. Although Romans 6:6 and Colossians 3:9 look at the definitive past act, the exhortations in the surrounding context urge us to put away sin in the present and live according to this past act. Accepting the tension between the past act (that which is indicated to be fact about us) and the present life (that which is now commanded of us) enables us to better understand the change from the old man in Adam to the new man in Christ.

The concept of living out who we really are is also seen in the apostle's exhortation, "Be transformed by the renewing of your mind" (Romans 12:2; see also 2 Corinthians 3:18). The word *transformed* refers to a change in which a person's true inner condition is shown outwardly. In the words of one commentator, "'form' at the heart of 'transformed' refers to what grows out of necessity from an inward condition."[27] This is illustrated for us in the *transfiguration* (same Greek root as *transformed*) of Jesus (Matthew 17:1-3). When the Lord was transfigured, there was no change in His nature. He was still fully God and fully man. Jesus was simply letting His true nature of deity shine through, or be manifested. Similarly, when Paul wrote about believers being "transformed," he was not talking about a change in who we really are. He was referring to us becoming outwardly (in our demeanor and behavior) what we really are in the depth of our being: new creations in Christ.

Putting on Christ

Putting on Christ is also a past and present matter. Paul says in Galatians 3:27, "All of you who were baptized into Christ have clothed yourselves with Christ." The Greek word translated "clothed yourselves" is the same word translated as "put on" in relation to the new man, or new self (see Ephesians 4:24; Colossians 3:10). Paul's phrase can be translated "you...have put on Christ."

To clothe oneself with, or to put on, a person "means to take on the characteristics, virtues, and/or intentions of the one referred to, and so to become like that person."[28] We became a partaker of the divine nature (2 Peter 1:4) and began the process of becoming like Him. God didn't simply give us the power to imitate Him; He actually reconciled us to Himself so that our soul is in union with His! In summary, we are to assume responsibility for becoming what we already are in Christ by the grace of God.

Dying and Rising with Christ

Every Christian has died with Christ and has been raised with Him, but in our growth experience we have not totally realized the fullness of these events. The pattern of Christ's death and resurrection is presented in Scripture as the essence of transformation. These events—through which we have passed in our inner person—now determine our life and behavior. To be transformed into the image of Christ or have Christ formed in us (Galatians 4:19) means that Christ effects in us what took place in Him.

The essence of sanctification is dying in order that we might live. This was the pathway of Christ; it is also the pathway to glory for the believer. We find an analogy of this in the new life that comes forth from every seed that is sown. If you wanted to grow a giant oak tree, what would you do? Plant an oak tree? No, you would plant an acorn. If you could watch the process, you would see that tiny acorn die to itself so that out of it could grow a majestic oak tree. If the acorn exists only for itself, it will never become what it was intended to be.

The seed to become what God intends us to be is sown in every child of God. Jesus said, "The hour has come for the Son of Man to be glorified. Truly, truly, I say to you, unless a grain of wheat falls into the earth and dies, it remains alone; but if it dies, it bears much fruit" (John 12:23-24). Like the caterpillar that voluntarily attaches itself to a tree in order to hang upside down (and then later to be "glorified" as a butterfly), we too must realize that the path upward is first downward. In order to be glorified, Jesus had first to die. We too have to die to who we were in Adam and give up all our dreams for self-glorification in the flesh and joyfully choose to glorify God in our bodies.

No Pain, No Gain

The problem is that "self" will never cast out "self." We have to be led to do that by the Holy Spirit. "We who are alive are always being given over to death for Jesus' sake, so that his life may be revealed in our mortal body" (2 Corinthians 4:11). There is a struggle to overcome sin even though we have already died to it. Such struggling may appear to be a negative thing, but it's actually to our benefit. Let us illustrate. If you saw a butterfly struggling to emerge from its cocoon, would you try to help it? That may seem to be the loving thing to do, but it isn't—because that struggle, in part, is what gives the butterfly the strength to fly. You would actually be interfering with the butterfly's potential to fly.

The same is true of a baby eagle emerging from its egg. Whether we walk among the turkeys or soar with the eagles in the heavenlies has much to do with our willingness to overcome the residual effects of our past. John writes, "He who overcomes will inherit all this, and I will be his God and he will be my son" (Revelation 21:7). "No pain, no gain" seems to be a principle of life. Therefore, "endure hardship as discipline; God is treating you as sons" (Hebrews 12:7).

If we didn't have a part to play in overcoming the power of sin, then we would all probably wallow in sin. That our spiritual growth is connected with our endeavors to overcome sin is evident in 1 John 2:12-14, where we read that "children" have overcome the *penalty* of sin, but the "young men" in the faith have overcome the evil one and the *power* of sin. Remember that the god of this world and the prince of the power of the air is roaring around like a hungry lion seeking someone to devour. Learning how to resist the devil and crucify the flesh is a critical part of growing in Christ. The flesh desires to sin, but our new nature in Christ desires to live righteously.

Because of our position in Christ we are no longer "in the flesh," but since the flesh remains after salvation, we can still choose to walk according to it (that is, we can choose to live as a natural person—the way we lived before we were born again). We summarize our situation in the following chart:

Who We Are

In Adam *(1 Corinthians 15:22a)*		In Christ *(1 Corinthians 15:22b)*
old man	*by ancestry*	new man
sinful (Ephesians 2:1-3)	*by nature*	partaker of the divine nature (2 Peter 1:4)
in the flesh (Romans 8:8)	*by birth*	in the Spirit (Romans 8:9)
walk after the flesh (Galatians 5:19-21)	*by choice*	walk after the Spirit (Galatians 5:22-23)

Love's Key Role in Sanctification

If a person were a fully sanctified child of God, that person's heart would be fully enlarged. He would be free from his past. He would be like Christ in His character—a character that is called "love" in the Bible. "The goal of our instruction is love from a pure heart and a good conscience and a sincere faith" (1 Timothy 1:5 NASB). The fact that God is love makes love the focus of our Christian life. Knowledge of God and union with Him through Christ means a life of love. Glenn Hinson comments on this:

> What can we do to attain purity of heart? The answer to this is: surrender, abandon ourselves, submit, yield, humble ourselves, give ourselves over to God. However apt we may be at education, self-understanding or formation, we cannot transform the impure into the pure, the sinful into the saintly, the unlovely into the lovely. God alone can do that. God's love alone can perform the miracle required. If we surrender, love will come in and cleanse and purify and transform.[29]

Jesus said, "A new command I give you: Love one another. As I have loved you, so you must love one another" (John 13:34). The obligation to love one another has always been recognized by all people. It was commanded in the Old Testament (Deuteronomy 6:5; Leviticus 19:18), and by the power of God was practiced to some extent by His people. But the revelation of its full meaning awaited Christ's giving Himself for us.

And only in Him can we fulfill His "new" command to love with the divine love with which He loved us. God loves us not because we are lovable, but because it is His nature to love us—"God is love" (1 John 4:8). That is why His love is unconditional. In contrast our natural "love" for one another is selective. Jesus remarked about this, "If you love those who love you, what credit is that to you? Even 'sinners' love those who love them" (Luke 6:32). However, the presence of God in our lives enables us to love as He does: "We love because He first loved us" (1 John 4:19). In other words, because we have become a partaker of the divine nature—which is love—we can by the grace of God love the unlovely.

The word "love" in Scripture is both a verb and a noun. When used as a noun (agape), it refers to the character of God, because He is love. For instance, "Love is patient, love is kind" (1 Corinthians 13:4) because He is patient and kind. When used as a verb (agapao), it describes the sacrificial actions taken by one who seeks to meet the needs of another: "God so loved the world that he gave his one and only Son" (John 3:16). Jesus demonstrated His love by sacrificing His life in order to meet our most urgent need. It could be said that the evidence of John 3:16 being fulfilled in our lives is described in 1 John 3:16-18:

> This is how we know what love is: Jesus Christ laid down his life for us. And we ought to lay down our lives for our brothers. If anyone has material possessions and sees his brother in need but has no pity on him, how can the love of God be in him? Dear children, let us not love with words or tongue but with actions and in truth.

The capacity to do loving things for other people springs from the nature and character of God within us. We are not first called to do what appear to be loving things for others; we are first called to be like Christ. Loving deeds flow out of our new life in Him.

Jesus said the greatest commandment is to

> "love the Lord your God with all your heart and with all your soul and with all your mind." This is the first and greatest commandment. And the second is like it: "Love your neighbor as yourself." All the Law and the Prophets hang on these two commandments (Matthew 22:37-40).

Love Is the Goal

These verses above portray love as the fulfillment of all of the commandments and the only basis for our righteous acts toward other people. When we are filled, or controlled, by the Spirit we will bear fruit, and the fruit of the Spirit is love (Galatians 5:22). Notice that the fruit of the Spirit is *singular* (*fruit*, not *fruits*)—love. The other traits listed in Galatians 5:22-23—joy, peace, patience, and so on—are characteristics of love. The characteristic of the new person (or the primary characteristic of sanctification) is love.

Love is the fulfillment of all ethical commands. It is not *doing* this or that, but *loving* so that the doing will flow. Paul notes, "He who loves his fellowman has fulfilled the law" (Romans 13:8). Peter Kreeft makes this observation:

> One of the things we mean when we say that love is the fulfillment of the law is that when we do not love a person, it is difficult or impossible to fulfill the moral law with respect to that person; but when we love someone, it is possible, even easy, even inevitable and positively delightful to do what the moral law commands us to do to him or her. It is

hard to do good deeds to one you despise, but joy to
do the same deeds to one you love.[30]

The contrast between the acts of the old nature (the flesh) and
the fruit of the Spirit is the difference between death and life.
Deeds done in the flesh, which has no life, are dead acts; fruit can
be produced only by something that is alive. The flesh can perform certain acts, but the fruit of the Spirit produces character.

To be perfected in love is the ultimate goal of being sanctified
in Christ. St. John of the Cross said, "In the twilight of our lives,
we will be judged on how we have loved."[31] Once we have fallen
in love with God and all that is true and good, we will naturally
(or better, supernaturally) fall in love with all others created in
His image. "Whoever loves God must also love his brother"
(1 John 4:21). His love simply compels us to do this.

The nature of godly love corresponds with becoming a new
self. As we die to the old self, we move away from a fleshly type
of love that loves others because of what they do for us. Such
"love" merely seeks to satisfy its own lusts. It is in reality a love
of self, which seeks to meet only its own needs. It is conditional
because it says, "I will love you if you will love me." Finally,
fleshly love is dependent upon its object. Sanctified love, in
contrast, is sacrificial and not dependent upon its object. Henry
Scougal captured that truth in the following words:

> Perfect love is a kind of self-dereliction, a wan-
> dering out of ourselves; it is a kind of voluntary
> death, wherein the lover dies to himself and all his
> own interests, not thinking of them nor caring for
> them any more, and minding nothing but how he
> may please and gratify the party whom he loves.
> Thus he is quite undone unless he meets with reci-
> procal affection; he neglects himself, and the other
> hath no regard to him; but if he be beloved, he is
> revived, as it were, and liveth in the soul and care of
> the person whom he loves; and now he begins to
> mind his own concernments, not so much because

they are his as because the beloved is pleased to own an interest in them. He becomes dear unto himself, because he is so unto the other.[32]

Overcoming the Presence of Sin

Scripture teaches that progressive sanctification—enlarging the heart—is making our position in Christ and the newness of our person through regeneration increasingly real in life. Naturally, this involves the process of turning from the attitude and practice of sin with all of their negative effects in life to that of the attitude and practice of righteousness with all of their positive effects.

Though sin no longer reigns over us, it can still dwell within us. John Calvin says that "sin ceases only to reign; it does not also cease to dwell in them [believers]. Accordingly, we say that the old man was so crucified, and the law of sin so abolished in the children of God, that some vestiges remain; not to rule over them, but to humble them by the consciousness of their own weakness."[33] John also makes it clear, in 1 John 1:7-10, that believers are still involved with sin:

> If we walk in the light, as he is in the light, we have fellowship with one another, and the blood of Jesus, his Son, purifies us from all sin. If we claim to be without sin, we deceive ourselves and the truth is not in us. If we confess our sins, he is faithful and just and will forgive us our sins and purify us from all unrighteousness. If we claim we have not sinned, we make him out to be a liar and his word has no place in our lives.

We are continually being cleansed from sin as we walk in the light. (We know that walking in the light cannot mean sinless perfection, because verse eight says we deceive ourselves if we say we have no sin.) It is a process of living in continuous and conscious moral agreement with our heavenly Father. It is essentially the same as *confessing*, which means "to agree with God." This passage gives no instruction to ask God for forgiveness—because we are already forgiven, but we do need to live honestly and openly before God. If it's necessary for believers to continually be cleansed from sin, then they must somehow have sin. Saying that we are without sin indicates that we do not have the truth in us. As Calvin put it, "There remains in a regenerate man a smoldering cinder of evil, from which desires continually leap forth to allure and spur him to commit sin."[34]

That sin is present in the new person is also affirmed in Paul's description of a continual battle going on in the believer: "I say, walk by the Spirit, and you will not carry out the desire of the flesh. For the flesh sets its desire against the Spirit, and the Spirit against the flesh; for these are in opposition to one another" (Galatians 5:16-17 NASB). The verb translated "sets its desire" is in the present tense, which indicates a continual ongoing antagonism between the "flesh" (the old tendency to live life independently of God) and the Spirit (who lives in us and seeks to lead us in holiness). Paul explains our combat against sin as continually "putting to death [present tense] the deeds of the body" (Romans 8:13 NASB).

To help us grow away from sin and toward Him, our heavenly Father disciplines us as His children so that we may share in His holiness and reap a harvest of righteousness and peace (Hebrews 12:5-11). We grow in holiness as we more and more put off sinful desires and their actions by the increasing daily realization of our newness and the truth that we really are alive in Christ—as revealed in the following passages taken from Neil's book *Victory Over the Darkness:*[35]

Who Am I?

Matthew 5:13	I am the salt of the earth.
Matthew 5:14	I am the light of the world.

John 1:12	I am a child of God (part of His family—see Romans 8:16).
John 15:1,5	I am part of the *true* vine, a channel (branch) of His (Christ's) life.
John 15:15	I am Christ's friend.
John 15:16	I am chosen and appointed by Christ to bear *His* fruit.
Romans 6:18	I am a slave of righteousness.
Romans 6:22	I am enslaved to God.
Romans 8:14-15	I am a son of God (see also Galatians 3:26 and 4:6).
Romans 8:17	I am a joint-heir with Christ, sharing His inheritance with Him.
1 Corinthians 3:16	I am a temple (home) of God. His Spirit (His life) dwells in me.
1 Corinthians 6:17	I am joined (united) to the Lord and am one spirit with Him.
1 Corinthians 12:27	I am a member (part) of Christ's body (see Ephesians 5:30).
2 Corinthians 5:17	I am a new creation (new person).
2 Corinthians 5:18	I am reconciled to God and am a minister of reconciliation.
Galatians 3:26,28	I am a son of God and one in Christ.
Galatians 4:6-7	I am an heir of God since I am a son of God.
Ephesians 1:1	I am a saint (see 1 Corinthians 1:2, Philippians 1:1, and Colossians 1:2).
Ephesians 2:6	I am seated with Christ in the heavenlies.
Ephesians 2:10	I am God's workmanship (handiwork) created (born anew) in Christ to do His work that He planned before-hand that I should do.

Ephesians 2:19	I am a fellow citizen with the rest of God's people in His family.
Ephesians 3:1; 4:1	I am a prisoner of Christ.
Ephesians 4:24	I am righteous and holy.
Philippians 3:20	I am a citizen of heaven.
Colossians 3:3	I am hidden with Christ in God.
Colossians 3:4	I am an expression of the life of Christ because He is my life.
Colossians 3:12	I am chosen of God, holy, and dearly loved.
1 Thessalonians 1:4	I am chosen and dearly loved by God.
1 Thessalonians 5:5	I am a son of light and not of darkness.
Hebrews 3:1	I am a holy brother, partaker of a heavenly calling.
Hebrews 3:14	I am a partaker of Christ...I share in His life.
1 Peter 2:5	I am one of God's living stones and am being built up (in Christ).
1 Peter 2:9-10	I am a member of a chosen race, a royal priesthood, a holy nation, a people for God's own possession to proclaim the excellencies of Him.
1 Peter 2:11	I am an alien and stranger to this world I temporarily live in.
1 Peter 5:8	I am an enemy of the devil.
1 John 3:1-2	I am now a child of God. I will resemble Christ when He returns.
1 John 5:18	I am born of God, and the evil one (the devil) cannot touch me.

I am not the great "I AM" (Exodus 3:14;
John 8:24,28,58), "but by the grace of God I am
what I am" (1 Corinthians 15:10).

QUESTIONS FOR THOUGHT
AND DISCUSSION

1. What is the difference between enlarging your heart and increasing in knowledge?

2. How can you incorporate the living Word into your heart?

3. What part of the Colossians 1:9-12 cycle do you find the hardest to process? Why?

4. What is the difference between that which is indicated to be fact about us (the indicative) and that which is commanded of us (the imperative)?

5. The epistles are about half indicative and half imperative. Do you see that balance being taught or modeled in Christian circles—that is, are we celebrating what has already been accomplished in equal balance with what we ought to do?

6. Why does God allow us to struggle with sin?

7. What should be the goal of our instruction?

8. Why does knowing our identity and position in Christ help us overcome sin?

CHAPTER SIX

The Responsibility for Growth

The greatest need of the world today is the spiritual power necessary for the overthrow of evil, for the establishment of righteousness, and for the ushering in of the era of perpetual peace; and that spiritual power begins in the surrender of the individual to God. It commences with obedience to the first commandment.

WILLIAM JENNINGS BRYAN

WHEN I (NEIL) WAS GROWING UP on a farm in Minnesota, spring was a busy season of preparing the ground and sowing seeds for harvest. One method of sowing was called *broadcasting*. We simply cast the seeds upon the surface of the earth. Some of the seeds never took root, but most did if it rained. To spread the seed, we used an end-gate seeder that we mounted on the tailgate of a wagon. A tractor pulled the wagon that did the broadcasting. This planting process required two people—one to drive the tractor, and one to sit in the wagon and keep the seeder filled.

Although the seeder did the actual broadcasting, the power to sow the seed was in the tractor, not the seeder. If the tractor stopped, so did the sowing. But the sowing also stopped if the seeder failed to work. If the latter happened, though, the tractor would still continue to supply the power and continue in the right direction toward the end of the row.

We have the privilege of sowing and cultivating, but God causes the increase. If we don't plant and water, nothing grows. God is the source of life, which is the power to grow. He also supplies the seed that we are called to sow: "He who supplies seed to the sower and bread for food will also supply and increase your store of seed and will enlarge the harvest of your righteousness" (2 Corinthians 9:10). Paul also observed,

> I planted the seed, Apollos watered it, but God made it grow. So neither he who plants nor he who waters is anything, but only God, who makes things grow. The man who plants and the man who waters have one purpose, and each will be rewarded according to his own labor. For we are God's fellow workers; you are God's field, God's building (1 Corinthians 3:6-9).

From germination to harvest, our sanctification is first and foremost the work of God. We have no natural resources in ourselves to overcome the power of sin still present in our lives. However, Scripture also teaches the need for us to assume our responsibility for the continuing process of sanctification. That is only logical since sanctification involves the change of our own self, which includes our thinking, our emotions, and our will.

There is a real distinction between what God has done and will continue to do, and what our responsibility is. We cannot do for ourselves what God has already done and will do for us. We can try to save ourselves, but it will do us no good. We can and should rest in the finished work of Christ, trust in the sovereign grace of God to be faithful to His Word, and have confidence that He will continue to be and do all that He has said He will be and do.

On the other hand, God will not do for us what He has called us to do. In a very real sense, He can't. He can only do that which is consistent with His holy nature, and He cannot deviate from His Word. There can be nothing but defeat and disappointment for Christians who expect God to do for them what He has commanded them to do. God has done all He needs to do in order for us to live a victorious Christian life. He has defeated the devil, forgiven our sins, and given us eternal life. He has equipped us with His Holy Spirit, and we are now seated with Christ in the heavenlies. From that position of authority over the kingdom of darkness we are to continue the work of Christ on planet Earth. Does the devil have to flee from us if we don't resist him? Probably not! You cannot passively take your place in Christ. You must "put on the full armor of God, so that when the day of evil comes, you may be able to stand your ground, and after you have done everything, to stand" (Ephesians 6:13).

When we fail to recognize what God holds us responsible for, we set ourselves up for disappointment because we will think that either God isn't at work in our lives or we are spiritual failures because things don't go the way we expect.

God the Father's Role in Our Sanctification

God is the primary agent of our sanctification because He is the only source of life, righteousness, love, and truth. Sanctification is the process of God sharing His life with and through us as shown in Paul's prayer: "May God himself, the God of peace, sanctify you through and through. May your whole spirit, soul and body be kept blameless at the coming of our Lord Jesus Christ. The one who calls you is faithful and he will do it" (1 Thessalonians 5:23-24). The truth that God is the primary agent of sanctification is also shown in 2 Peter 1:3-9, which goes into specific detail about God's role and our responsibility.

What God has done:

His divine power has given us everything we need
for life and godliness through our knowledge of him

who called us by his own glory and goodness. Through these he has given us his very great and precious promises, so that through them you may participate in the divine nature and escape the corruption in the world caused by evil desires (verses 3-4).

What we must do:

For this very reason, make every effort to add to your faith goodness; and to goodness, knowledge; and to knowledge, self-control; and to self-control, perseverance; and to perseverance, godliness; and to godliness, brotherly kindness; and to brotherly kindness, love. For if you possess these qualities in increasing measure, they will keep you from being ineffective and unproductive in your knowledge of our Lord Jesus Christ. But if anyone does not have them, he is nearsighted and blind, and has forgotten that he has been cleansed from his past sins (verses 5-9).

God has given us everything we need for life and godliness. He has equally distributed Himself to all His children, and every Christian has been made a partaker of His divine nature. Our responsibility is to make every effort to add on to our faith the character qualities of goodness, knowledge, self-control, perseverance, godliness, brotherly kindness, and love. If we do so, we will live effective and productive lives. The people who don't do this have forgotten that they are alive in Christ and dead to sin. What should they do then? Try harder? No! They should affirm again their faith foundation of who they are in Christ and commit themselves to their growth in character: "Brethren, be all the more diligent to make certain about His calling and choosing you; for as long as you practice these things, you will never stumble" (2 Peter 1:10 NASB).

All that we have received from God has eternal value. "We are God's workmanship" (Ephesians 2:10), and "his incomparably great power" (1:19) is at work in us to produce a new creation. The same Greek word translated "workmanship" is frequently used in the Septuagint (a Greek translation of the Old Testament produced before Christ's time on Earth) to refer to creation as God's "work." Paul says in Romans 14:20 that believers are "the work of God." Sanctification is the increasing experience of spiritual and eternal life, of which God is the only source (see Psalm 36:9; John 17:3; Ephesians 4:18).

The book of Hebrews tells us about a further role the Father plays. We are exhorted, "Endure hardship as discipline; God is treating you as sons. For what son is not disciplined by his father?…Our fathers disciplined us for a little while as they thought best; but God disciplines us for our good, that we may share in his holiness" (12:7,10). God does not punish us for doing something wrong; He disciplines us for our good, which reinforces our position as His sons.

While God the Father is the originating agent in our sanctification, Christ and the Holy Spirit also play roles in our sanctification. As we would expect, all three members of the Trinity have a part in making us holy.

Christ's Role in Our Sanctification

At the moment of salvation, believers are joined to Christ so that He is their life. The often repeated prepositional phrases "in Christ," "in Him," and "in the beloved" all mean that our souls are in union with God. Each phrase teaches that we are right now "alive in Christ." Every aspect of Christian work and service is dependent upon this truth because apart from Christ we can do nothing. Paul points to this in his own work: "I have sent to you Timothy, who is my beloved and faithful child in the Lord, and he will remind you of *my ways which are in Christ, just as I teach everywhere in every church*" (1 Corinthians 4:17 NASB). Richard Longenecker expands on this:

In Pauline parlance, that reality of personal commu-
nion between Christians and God is expressed from
the one side of the equation as being "in Christ," "in
Christ Jesus/Jesus Christ," "in him," or "in the Lord"…
[some 172 times including the pastoral epistles].

Viewed from the other side of the equation, the
usual way for Paul to express that relation between
God and his own is by some such phrase as "Christ
by his Spirit" or "the Spirit of God" or simply "the
Spirit" dwelling "in us" or "in you," though a few
times he says directly "Christ in me" ([2:20;] cf.
Colossians 1:27,29; see also Ephesians 3:16,17) or
"Christ in you" (cf. the interchange of expressions in
Romans 8:9-11).[36]

For every verse that says *Christ is in you,* there are approxi-
mately ten verses that say *you are in Christ.* According to Robert
Tannehill, the phrase "in Christ" refers to "action or existence as
it is characterized by a particular power, the power of Christ and
his saving acts."[37] There are no verses in the Bible that instruct us
to pursue power, because we already have all the power we need
in Christ. The problem is, we don't know it—so Paul wrote in
Ephesians 1:18-19, "I pray also that the eyes of your heart may be
enlightened in order that you may know the hope to which he has
called you, the riches of his glorious inheritance in the saints,
and his incomparably great power for us who believe."

Pursuing something you already have can only lead you
down the wrong road. Power for the Christian is found in the
truth, and the power of the devil is in the lie. If you expose
Satan's lies, you will destroy his hold on people, because he
truly is a defeated foe. Satan has deceived the whole world
(Revelation 12:9); consequently, the world lies in the power of
the evil one (1 John 5:19). Satan can do nothing about your
position in Christ, but if he can get you to believe that your
position in Christ isn't for real or for you, then you will live as
though it isn't.

A Walk "in Christ"

Progressive sanctification is a walk with God "in Christ." Jesus invited us to walk with Him: "Come to me, all you who are weary and burdened, and I will give you rest. Take my yoke upon you and learn from me, for I am gentle and humble in heart, and you will find rest for your souls. For my yoke is easy and my burden is light" (Matthew 11:28-30). Jesus didn't say to come to the synagogue or submit to some program. He said, "Come to Me"—come to My presence, and I will give you rest. There is a "Sabbath-rest for the people of God; for anyone who enters God's rest also rests from his own work" (Hebrews 4:9-10). This much-needed rest in the Lord is not an abdication of our responsibility nor a cessation of labor. Rather, it is practicing the presence of God and living by faith in the power of the Holy Spirit.

Jesus often used illustrations that the people of His day could relate to. He was especially familiar with illustrations and metaphors related to carpentry, for He was raised in the home of a carpenter. Carpenters in those days fashioned yokes and doors, both of which the Lord used to speak of Himself. The yoke referred to in Matthew 11:28-30 was a heavy wooden beam that fit over the shoulders of two oxen. The only way the yoke could work was if both oxen were in it and pulling together. If only one tried to use the yoke, it would be a chafing and binding affair.

Farmers break in a new ox by placing it in a yoke with an older, seasoned ox who has learned obedience from the things he has suffered (see Hebrews 5:8). The older ox knows he has a whole day of work ahead, and he knows better than to run when he should be walking. He also knows better than to stray off to the left or to the right, since such sidetracks only lead to more work later on down the path.

The young ox may think the pace is a little slow and try to run ahead, but he will only burn out before noon. The young ox will also get a sore neck if he is tempted to stray off to the left or the right. If the young ox has any sense, he will start to realize that maybe the older ox knows what he is doing.

So it is as we share the yoke with Christ. It is always best to slow down and learn from the One who knows where He is going and how to get there. You will learn from Christ to take one day at a time and learn the priority of relationships and the graceful ways of God.

> Do you not know? Have you not heard? The LORD is the everlasting God, the Creator of the ends of the earth. He will not grow tired or weary, and his understanding no one can fathom. He gives strength to the weary and increases the power of the weak. Even youths grow tired and weary, and young men stumble and fall; but those who hope in the LORD will renew their strength. They will soar on wings like eagles; they will run and not grow weary, they will walk and not be faint (Isaiah 40:28-31).

The Holy Spirit's Role in Our Sanctification

Paul also attributes the continuing process of sanctification to the Holy Spirit (1 Thessalonians 4:3-8). In verse 3 it is stated that God has called us to "be sanctified." In verses 7-8 we read that God has called us not to be impure "but to live a holy life." Verse 8 then goes on to connect the presence of the Holy Spirit to Paul's discussion about our sanctification: "He who rejects this instruction does not reject man but God, who gives you his Holy Spirit."

The connection of the Spirit to progressive sanctification is also implied in many other references. In Galatians 5:22-23, the actual fruit of sanctification is said to be produced by the Spirit and the love of God is poured into our lives through the Spirit (Romans 5:5). The requirements of the law are worked through the Spirit (Romans 8:4), it is by the Spirit we put to death the misdeeds of the body (8:13-14), and we are renewed by the Spirit (Titus 3:5).

Concerned that He was leaving His disciples behind to carry on His ministry in a fallen world, Jesus asked the Father, "My prayer is not that you take them out of the world but that you protect them from the evil one. They are not of the world, even as I am not of it. Sanctify them by the truth; your word is truth" (John 17:15-17). It is the Holy Spirit who leads us into all truth (16:13). This is the great work of the Holy Spirit, who is first and foremost "the Spirit of truth" (14:17). Truth is the means by which we are sanctified.

Since it could be said that the Father is the initiator of sanctification, and that Christ is the mediator whose saving work in death and resurrection provides the basis for our sanctification, of the Holy Spirit it could be said that He is the One who actually comes into all creation to sustain and enliven it. He indwells the believer to apply the sanctifying work of Christ and bring personal union with all the members of the Trinity.

Our Role in Our Sanctification

Since we are what we are only by the grace of God, and since He is the primary agent of our sanctification, should we simply "let go and let God" make us holy? Scripture clearly teaches that this is not the case. It gives us a role in our sanctification. Paul wrote in Philippians 2:12-13, "Continue to work out *your* salvation with fear and trembling, for it is God who works in you to will and to act according to his good purpose." The Greek word for "work out" (*katergazomai*) means "to bring about, produce, create." Bible commentator Moses Silva says, "It is impossible to tone down the force with which Paul here points to our conscious activity in sanctification…Our salvation, which we confess to be God's from beginning to end, is here described as something that we must bring about."[38]

In this process of "working out," Paul describes himself as a runner:

Brothers, I do not consider myself yet to have taken hold of it. But one thing I do: Forgetting what is behind and straining toward what is ahead, I press on toward the goal to win the prize for which God has called me heavenward in Christ Jesus (Philippians 3:13-14).

This goal or prize is the completion of our sanctification.

Doing Our Part

There was a pastor who found great joy in gardening. On a rare day off, one of his deacons found him working in his garden. "My, the Lord sure gave you a beautiful garden," he said to the pastor. The pastor responded, "Well, thank you very much, but you should have seen it when God had it to Himself!" When it comes to sowing and harvesting for God's kingdom, the Lord in His sovereignty has chosen to allow us to participate in His work.

Believers have something in common with electrical appliances. Every appliance is created for a specific purpose, but none can accomplish anything without electricity. They come in all shapes and colors, but they will never fulfill their purpose unless they receive power from a generating station. By themselves they don't even make good furniture or decoration for the house. But with the flip of a switch they are all energized in order to fulfill their purpose. The toaster makes toast, the coffeemaker brews coffee, and the refrigerator preserves food. It would be foolish to say one appliance is better than the other, for they were all designed with a different purpose in mind.

We are not supposed to keep our work hidden. The Lord will receive no glory if we don't do good deeds or let our light shine. Neither will He receive any glory if we draw attention to ourselves by trying to find some meaningful existence without being plugged in. Jesus said,

You are the light of the world. A city on a hill cannot be hidden. Neither do people light a lamp and put it under a bowl. Instead they put it on its stand, and it gives light to everyone in the house. In the same way, let your light shine before men, that they may see your good deeds and praise your Father in heaven (Matthew 5:14-16).

A Combined Effort

How much will be accomplished to the glory of God in this present church age if we try to do everything by ourselves? Nothing! How much will be accomplished if we sit back in some "holy piety" and expect God to do it all? Apparently nothing, because God has committed Himself to work through the church. Paul explained,

His intent was that now, *through the church*, the manifold wisdom of God should be made known to the rulers and authorities in the heavenly realms, according to his eternal purpose which he accomplished in Christ Jesus our Lord. In him and through faith in him we may approach God with freedom and confidence (Ephesians 3:10-12).

We cannot passively take our place in Christ, nor can we passively stand against the evil one. We are told to "put on the Lord Jesus Christ, and make no provision for the flesh in regard to its lusts" (Romans 13:14 NASB). What if we don't actively put on Christ? What if we do make provision for the flesh? We are told to put on the armor of God; what if we don't? We are told not to use our bodies as instruments of unrighteousness (Romans 6:12-13). What if we do? We are told to take every thought captive to the obedience of Christ (2 Corinthians 10:5); what if we don't? At best we will surely stop bearing fruit, and at worst we will be utterly defeated.

Because God Works, We Work

We are saved by faith and sanctified by faith, but according to James, faith without works is dead:

> What good is it, my brothers, if a man claims to have faith but has no deeds? Can such faith save him?...Faith by itself, if it is not accompanied by action, is dead. But someone will say, "You have faith; I have deeds." Show me your faith without deeds, and I will show you my faith by what I do (2:14,17-18).

Therefore, if a person is truly a Christian, it will be demonstrated by how he or she lives. What a person does is a reflection of what he or she has chosen to believe.

In the process of sanctification, we are yoked together with Christ, and we must pull together under His direction and by His power. It is inappropriate to speak of *synergism*—that is, God does part and man does part. God's work is always initiatory and primary, and our work is dependent upon Him. John Murray explains this relationship:

> God's working in us is not suspended because we work, nor our working suspended because God works. Neither is the relation strictly one of cooperation, as if God did his part and we did ours so that the conjunction or coordination of both produced the required result. God works and we also work. But the relation is that because God works, we work. All working out of salvation on our part is the effect of God's working in us...We have here not only the explanation of all acceptable activity on our part, but we also have the incentive to our willing and working...The more persistently active we are in working, the more persuaded we may be that all the energizing grace and power is of God.[39]

According to Ephesians 2:10, our good works are already prepared, but we must walk in them. Karl Barth commented on this passage, "The distinctive thing about Christian or theological ethics is that we do not have to do any carrying without remembering that we are carried."[40] The fact that God's work is prior and primary means that sanctification is ultimately a matter of faith, just as justification is. We are not departing from the sphere of faith when we move from justification to sanctification. We are not justified by faith and then sanctified by works. If we took that route, Paul would rise out of his grave and say again,

> You foolish Galatians! Who has bewitched you?...I would like to learn just one thing from you: Did you receive the Spirit by observing the law, or by believing what you heard? Are you so foolish? After beginning with the Spirit, are you now trying to attain your goal by human effort? (Galatians 3:1-3).

What Christ Does and What We Do

Jesus' sinless life and His death were *for* us as a substitute. But the Spirit's work in applying the fruit of Christ's substitution is *not* done as a substitute. God does not will and do *for* us—rather, He works *in* us to will and to do (see Philippians 2:13). Therefore, we must actively exercise our will and do good works. For the Spirit to actually perform the work of sanctification without the person's active involvement ("substitutionary sanctification") would entail the mystical absorption of the human person into God and destroy the individual. If it is Christ or the Spirit doing everything, then there is no human person left.

The truth of what Paul says in Galatians 2:20 ("I no longer live, but Christ lives in me") cannot be interpreted as saying that Christ lives my life *instead* of me. Somehow Christ lives in me, and yet I also actively live. Paul continues, "The life I live in the body, I live by faith in the Son of God, who loved me and gave himself for me" (Galatians 2:20). The "I" that continues to live is still intact—but is now complete in Christ. Sanctification is actually the restoration of true selfhood. It calls the human faculties of personhood (mind, emotion, and will) into action so that they may be exercised and grow in holiness. God does not trample on our humanness—He sets us free in Christ to be fully human.

What we are saying is that our thinking, our feeling, and our willing are part of us. These capacities must be renewed in sanctification. God cannot renew us without working through them, which means that they must be active. Thus we must believe and obey by thinking, choosing, and feeling. These faculties of ours cannot be carried along passively, for then part of us is not functioning and is thus left out of our total renewal.

Sanctification Involves the Whole Person

The prophet Ezekiel challenged his listeners to "get a new heart and a new spirit" (Ezekiel 18:31), yet he still knew that people are dependent on God for this to happen. God Himself said in Ezekiel 11:19, "I will give them an undivided heart and put a new spirit in them; I will remove from them their heart of stone and give them a heart of flesh." Later, in 36:26, He said, "I will give you a new heart and put a new spirit in you." From these passages we can clearly see that the new heart and spirit are gifts from God, and yet we are called to have a part in receiving these gifts.

Jeremiah prophetically brings together our relationship with God and His gift of a new heart in Jeremiah 24:7: "I will give them a heart to know me, that I am the LORD. They will be my people, and I will be their God, for they will return to me with all their heart." This is a heart to know or experience God.

In the new covenant, under which every child of God is privileged to be, the Lord says,

I will put My law within them, and on their heart I will write it; and I will be their God, and they shall be My people. They will not teach again, each man his neighbor and each man his brother, saying, "Know the LORD," for they will all know Me, from the least of them to the greatest of them" (Jeremiah 31:33-34 NASB).

Therefore, "May the Lord direct your hearts into God's love and Christ's perseverance" (2 Thessalonians 3:5).

GOD IS THE PRIMARY AGENT of our sanctification because He gave us a new heart so that we would turn toward Him. When we do, we become an agent in our own sanctification, and our whole person is conformed to the image of God. Then we begin to love Him and others, as Henri Nouwen explained:

Somehow during the centuries we have come to believe that what makes us human is our mind...But Adam [a severely mentally handicapped person] keeps telling me over and over again that what makes us human is not our mind but our heart, not our ability to think but our ability to love. Whoever speaks about Adam as a vegetable or an animal-like creature misses the sacred mystery that Adam is fully capable of receiving and giving love. He is fully human, not a little bit human, not half human, not nearly human, but fully, completely human because he is all heart. And it is our heart that is made in the image and likeness of God.[41]

QUESTIONS FOR THOUGHT
AND DISCUSSION

1. Ultimately, who is responsible for our sanctification?

2. Distinguish between God's role and our role in sanctification.

3. Why must God discipline us?

4. What does it mean to be yoked with Christ?

5. How can we cooperate with God in order to be fully sanctified?

6. Are we saved by faith and then sanctified by our good works? Explain.

7. What would be some of the negative consequences if we expected God to "do it all"? If we tried to do it all by ourselves?

CHAPTER SEVEN

Transformed by
the Renewing of the Mind

It does not take a great mind to be a Christian,
but it takes all the mind a person has.

RICHARD C. RAINES

AN UNDERGRADUATE STUDENT at a Christian university was referred to me (Neil) for counseling by the chairman of her department. I was told she wasn't going to make it through the semester if she didn't get some help. She couldn't concentrate on her work, and her countenance revealed total defeat. She came from a Mormon family that had been split down the middle when her mother realized, after much searching and diligent study, that Joseph Smith was a false prophet. After following her mother's lead in making a decision for Christ, she enrolled in a good Christian college. Her first year had gone well, but now she found herself in a spiritual battle for her mind.

After hearing her story, I realized that she had not fully come to terms with her past. So I led her through a comprehensive process of repentance using the Steps to Freedom in Christ.* Her greatest struggle was facing the false beliefs and religious

---

*Freedom in Christ Ministries has found the Steps to be an excellent means of helping people completely submit to God through repentance and claim their freedom in Jesus Christ. See the appendix for more information.

practices of her Mormon family. Finally she chose the truth and renounced all the religious ceremonies she had participated in, such as baptizing and marrying for the dead. The dramatic change in her countenance revealed that the truth had set her free. I encouraged her to visit the restroom to freshen up and take a good look at herself in the mirror. "Why? Do I look that bad?" she asked. "No," I responded, "you look that good!" My secretary accompanied her and told me later that when the young woman had looked in the mirror, she had said in astonishment, "Why, I'm pretty!"

Repentance and Putting Off the Old Man

Renewing our mind begins with genuine repentance. John the Baptist preached, "Repent and believe the good news!" (Mark 1:15). The New Testament word "repentance" (Greek, *metanoeo*) is a combination of *meta*—which means "after," thus implying change—and *noeo*, which means "to perceive." *Noeo* comes from the root word *nous*, which is usually translated "mind." Repentance, then, literally means a change of mind, but in Scripture this means more than just a change of intellectual thought. It is a change of disposition or attitude. Thus repentance implies a change that affects the whole person. This is illustrated in Matthew 3:7-8, when the Pharisees and Sadducees came to be baptized by John. "He said to them: 'You brood of vipers! Who warned you to flee from the coming wrath? Produce fruit in keeping with repentance.'" John discerned that their repentance was not genuine. They wanted the blessings of God without giving up their habits, traditions, customs, worldly positions, and religious practices.

In the first weeks after Pentecost, Peter preached, "Repent, then, and turn to God, so that your sins may be wiped out, that times of refreshing may come from the Lord" (Acts 3:19). Paul said to Agrippa, "I preached that they should repent and turn to God and prove their repentance by their deeds" (Acts 26:20). The Lord doesn't want "anyone to perish, but everyone to come to repentance" (2 Peter 3:9). In the early church, coming to the Lord through saving faith included repenting from previous sinful beliefs and behaviors. Early postapostolic church history tells us that converts would stand, face the west, and make the following public declaration: "I renounce you, Satan, and all your works and all your ways."

The need for repentance continues in the believer's life even after coming to salvation. In the letters to the churches in the book of Revelation, again and again the risen Lord calls for His people to repent of false beliefs and sinful attitudes and actions. "Repent and do the things you did at first" (2:5). "Those whom I love I rebuke and discipline. So be earnest, and repent" (3:19; cf. 2:16; 3:3). Paul rejoiced that the Corinthian believers had come to a "godly sorrow" over their old sinful behavior, which led to repentance (2 Corinthians 7:9-10).

Repentance is the first step in renewing our minds. Without repentance, the effects of the old self are still in our minds. Progressive sanctification is stalled because we are still believing the lies of this world while at the same time professing to believe the truth. Christians who express their faith in God, but manifest no substantial change in their lives, are caught between two kingdoms. They are actually in the kingdom of light, but they are still believing the father of lies.

Reprogramming Our Minds

However, the truth will set us free and transform our character by the power of God. To understand how, we need to start by realizing that a greater transformation took place when we were born again spiritually than will take place when we die physically. Salvation isn't addition; it is transformation. As Christians, we are both physically and spiritually alive. When we die physically, we will be absent from the body and present with the Lord. Our tired old physical bodies will return to dust, and we will receive resurrected bodies, for "flesh and blood cannot inherit the kingdom of God" (1 Corinthians 15:50).

Until then, Paul urges us not to use our bodies as instruments of unrighteousness (Romans 6:12-14), because if we do we will allow sin to reign there. We are urged by the mercies of God to present our bodies to Him as living sacrifices (Romans 12:1). Paul then admonishes us to be transformed by the renewing of our minds (verse 2). Why? Because our minds were programmed to live independently of God. In progressive sanctification, we have to assume our responsibility to reprogram our minds with the truth of God's Word.

Like a computer, our brains record the experiences we have in life. Newborn babies come into this world with a clean slate in regard to memories. The only world they know is what they can see, hear, feel, taste, and smell. No personal experiences have been programmed into their "computer." Because they do not have the presence of God in their lives, however, their computers are bent to record all of their experiences in relation to self rather than God. As a result, during their early and formative years they learn to live independently of God.

When we come to Christ, our minds are still programmed to live independently of God. There is no "delete" or "clear" button that can be pushed to get rid of old thinking patterns; hence the need to renew (reprogram) our minds.

The flesh includes both the underlying inclination toward the lie "I am my own god," and the lies that have been inculcated into the mind by living in this fallen world. Both influence the attitude and activity of the person. Our fleshly programming processes all information from the perspective of life that is lived apart from God. It attempts to make sense of life without including God.

More Than Just New Thoughts

As fallen humans, we need more than just different thoughts, we need a new operating system as well—one that has a bent toward God and His truth. What is reprogrammed by God at the new birth is not the flesh, but the mind or the reasoning capacity, which can be dominated either by the flesh or the

Spirit. In order for the mind to function as God created it, the flesh with its manifestations (thoughts and behavior) must be crucified because they are in opposition to God. The committed saint has "crucified the flesh with its passions and desires" (Galatians 5:24 NASB). This was done in principle when we received Christ, but needs to be reaffirmed daily.

It takes time to renew our minds and replace the lies we have believed with the truth of God's Word. Yet that should not discourage us, for we have all the resources we need to make that happen. The Lord has given us the Holy Spirit, who is the Spirit of Truth (John 14:17), and He will guide us into all truth (John 16:13). Also, because we are one with God, "we have the mind of Christ" (1 Corinthians 2:16). Finally, Paul tells us we have superior weaponry available to us for winning the battle for our minds:

> Though we live in the world, we do not wage war as the world does. The weapons we fight with are not the weapons of the world. On the contrary, they have divine power to demolish strongholds. We demolish arguments and every pretension that sets itself up against the knowledge of God, and we take captive every thought to make it obedient to Christ (2 Corinthians 10:3-5).

Paul is not talking about defensive armor; he's talking about battering-ram weaponry that tears down strongholds that have been raised up against the knowledge of God.

Mental Strongholds

A stronghold is a negative pattern of thinking that has been burned into our minds either by habitual reinforcement or because of certain traumas we have experienced. How are strongholds erected in our minds? There is general agreement among developmental theorists that our vocabulary, worldview, and attitudes about life are assimilated primarily from the environment in which we are raised. Our temperaments and personalities are basically established by the time we are six years old.

This programming of our minds takes place in two ways. The first is through prevailing experiences we have in early childhood—such as the family we were raised in, the churches we went to—or didn't go to—the neighborhoods where we grew up, the communities we belonged to, and the friends that we had, or didn't have.

However, it isn't just the environment that determines how we develop. Two children can be raised in the same home, have the same parents, eat the same food, have the same friends, go to the same church, and respond differently. Admittedly, because they are two different individuals, their relationship to these various elements in their environment will inevitably have some differences. Nevertheless, every child interprets the world they live in from his or her own perspective. God has created each of us unique—in a way that He planned even before the foundation of the world (Ephesians 1:4; 2:10). Jacob and Esau came from the same womb, but they were very different in their temperament and personality.

Traumatic experiences are the second greatest contributor to the development of strongholds. For instance, you may have been raped when you were a child; you may have had parents who didn't get along and are divorced; or perhaps someone close to you died unexpectedly. These kinds of experiences are not assimilated into our minds over time; rather, they are burned into our minds because of their intensity.

As we struggle to reprogram our minds, we are also confronted daily with a world system that is not godly. Remember that Paul warned us, "Do not conform any longer to the pattern of this world" (Romans 12:2). Obviously we can continue, even as Christians, to allow the world we live in to affect our minds. That is why Paul also warned us, "See to it that no one takes you captive through hollow and deceptive philosophy, which depends on human tradition and the basic principles of this world rather than on Christ" (Colossians 2:8).

Even though we have the Spirit of truth to lead us, we can still choose to follow the ways of the world. The right and the responsibility to choose is the greatest power we possess, other than the presence of God in our lives. We can choose to pray or not to pray, to read our Bible or to read books that aren't edifying. Every child of God can choose to walk by the Spirit or to walk by the flesh (our old nature).

Dealing with Temptation

Because we live in this world, we are always going to face the reality of temptation. Keep in mind, however, that it's not a sin to be tempted. If that were so, then the worst sinner who ever lived would be Jesus, because He "has been tempted in every way, just as we are—yet was without sin" (Hebrews 4:15).

When Satan wants to tempt you, he knows which buttons to push! He knows our weaknesses. What may tempt one person may not tempt another. Satan's goal with temptation is to get us to live our lives independently of God—that is, to walk according to the flesh rather than the Spirit (see Galatians 5:16-23).

We can't deal with temptation by simply shutting ourselves off from the world. Even if we tried to do it, we would still face temptation. There is so much junk already programmed into our memory banks that we could be tempted for years without having to leave our homes! This is especially true in the area of sexual temptation. Once sexual strongholds are formulated in the mind, the mental impressions are there for instant recall.

If we are going to take the "way of escape" God has provided for us, we must take our thoughts captive to the obedience of Christ. If we allow our minds to ruminate on tempting thoughts, we will eventually take a path that, according to James, leads to sin and death:

> When tempted, no one should say, "God is tempting me." For God cannot be tempted by evil, nor does he tempt anyone; but each one is tempted when, by his own evil desire, he is dragged away and enticed. Then, after desire has conceived, it gives birth to

sin; and sin, when it is full-grown, gives birth to death (1:13-15).

The Mind and the New Self

To better understand how temptation affects us, refer to the diagram on page 113. Scripture says we have an outer man and an inner man (2 Corinthians 4:16). The outer person is our physical body, which relates to the world. Our physical brain is a part of the outer person. Our mind, on the other hand, is a part of the inner person. There is a fundamental difference between our brain and our mind: Our brain is organic matter. When we die physically, our brain will return to dust. We will be absent from the body and present with the Lord—but we will not be mindless.

It would only make sense that God would create the outer person to work together with the inner person. The obvious correspondence between the mind and the brain makes up a very sophisticated computer operation. The brain is hardware. It functions like a digital computer that has billions of switching transistors that code all the information in a binary numbering system of 0's and 1's. In a similar fashion, every neuron operates like a switch that turns on and off. Each neuron has many inputs (dendrites) and only one output, which channels the 40-plus different types of neurotransmitters to other dendrites. Millions upon millions of these make up the computer hardware, or the brain.

Our mind, on the other hand, represents the software. As the brain receives data from the external world through the five senses of the body, the mind acts as the compiler and chooses to interpret the data in the way it has been programmed. Until we come to Christ, our mind has been programmed by external sources and internal choices made without the knowledge of God or the benefit of His presence.

The tendency is to assume that mental and emotional problems are primarily caused by faulty hardware—the brain. There is no question that organic brain syndrome, Alzheimer's disease,

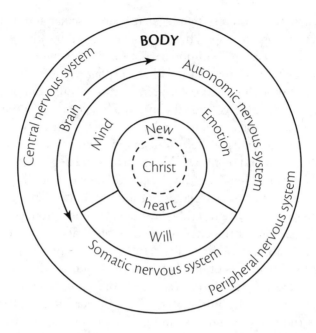

or lesser organic problems such as chemical or hormonal imbalances can impede our ability to function. Not too much can be done to correct faulty hardware—brains—and the best software program won't work if the computer is turned off or in disrepair. However, our primary problem is not the hardware, it is the software. Though we can do little to fix the hardware other than submitting our bodies to God as a living sacrifice and taking care of ourselves physically, we *can* change the software. Now that we are alive in Christ, we have been given the mind of Christ, a new heart, and the Holy Spirit to lead us into all truth.

How Our Thoughts Affect Us

The brain and the spinal cord make up the central nervous system, which branches out into the *peripheral* nervous system (as shown in the diagram above). The peripheral nervous system has two channels: the *autonomic* and the *somatic* nervous systems.

The somatic nervous system regulates our muscular and skeletal movements, such as speech, gestures, and so on. In other words, that which we have volitional control over—where we make choices. This system works together with our will.

Our autonomic nervous system regulates our glands, over which we have no volitional control. They function automatically. In a general sense, we don't have direct volitional control over our emotions either. You cannot will yourself to like someone you find repulsive. We do, however, have control over what we think—and we *can* decide to believe that what God says is true. Just as our glands are ultimately regulated by our central nervous system, so also are our emotions a product of our thoughts. It is not the circumstances of life that determine how we feel. Rather, how we feel is basically determined by how we interpret the events of life. Between the external stimulus (the event) and our emotional response is our brain (the receiver) and our mind (the interpreter). That is, our brain and mind assess the world around us, and our emotions respond to that information.

Let's apply all of this to the problem of stress. When external pressures put demands on our physical system, our adrenal glands respond by secreting cortisone-like hormones into our physical body. This is the natural "fight or flight" response to the pressures of life. If the pressures persist too long and our adrenal glands can't keep up, then our stress becomes *distress*. The result can be physical illness—or we may become irritable about things that wouldn't bother us physically or emotionally in less stressful times.

Why is it that two people can respond differently to the same stressful situation? Some actually thrive under pressure, while others fall apart. What is the difference between them? Do some people have superior adrenal glands? We don't think so. Although every person differs considerably in his or her physical makeup, the major difference isn't in the external factors. We all face the pressures of deadlines, schedules, trauma, and temptations. The major difference is in the software—how we mentally interpret the external world and process the data our brain is receiving.

When we encounter a difficulty, our minds can choose to respond by trusting God with the assurance of victory...or by viewing ourselves as the helpless victim of circumstances. The Israelite soldiers saw Goliath in reference to themselves and became stressed out. Young David saw the same giant in reference to God, and he triumphed in the same situation that had left experienced soldiers in defeat.

Faith in God and our knowledge of God's Word greatly affects how we interpret and respond to the pressures of this world. No matter what happens in life, we can always rest in the assurance that "in all things God works for the good of those who love him, who have been called according to his purpose" (Romans 8:28).

The Power of Choice

Our ability to choose applies to the area of sexual temptation. Our sex glands are part of our autonomic nervous system. They regulate normal sexual functioning according to our sexual identities. For instance, women don't control their menstrual cycle (though many record it). Our God-given sexual functioning and identity are not the cause of a lack of sexual self-control. In other words, our sex glands are not the cause of sexual immorality. But if we load up our minds with pornographic images and use our bodies as instruments of unrighteousness, we will drive our sex glands into overload. We *do* have control over what we choose to think, believe, and consequently do.

When we allow our minds to be stimulated externally, or by recalling experiences that we have had, an autonomic signal causes a hormone called *epinephrine* to be secreted into the bloodstream, which locks into our memory whatever stimulus is present at the time of the emotional excitement. This reaction causes us to involuntarily remember emotionally charged events—negative and traumatic ones as well as positive ones. That is why pornographic images and sexual experiences can remain in our memories for months and even years, whereas boring academic facts we've had to study can fade from our minds almost before the final exam is over! The positive benefit of this is that thinking of good memories can help result in a positive mood elevation.[42]

In every tempting situation we have a choice. We can respond according to the flesh (the way we learned to respond before we came to Christ), or we can respond according to the Spirit. Galatians 5:17 tells us the two are in opposition to each other because the flesh is programmed to live independently of God and the Holy Spirit is dependent upon God the Father. How do you know which one you have chosen? "The deeds of the flesh are evident" (Galatians 5:19-21 NASB), and so is "the fruit of the Spirit" (Galatians 5:22-23). Our countenance and behavior reveal the choices that we have made.

Suppose you choose to walk "according to the elementary principles of the world, rather than according to Christ" (Colossians 2:8 NASB). If you continue to do that for about six weeks, you will establish a habit that leads to the formation of a stronghold—burned into your mind by the habitual reinforcement of an external stimulus. The result is something less than a Christlike temperament.

Mental strongholds are sometimes called *flesh patterns*, and the concept is very similar to what psychologists call *defense mechanisms*. For instance, feelings of inferiority are a stronghold that many Christians struggle with. How do they develop an inferiority complex? Are they born with it? No, it develops over time because of the pressures foisted upon them by the performance-based world they live in. Not everybody gets perfect grades or makes the football team or wins the beauty contest. Does that mean they truly are inferior? The world system would have them believe they are, but God doesn't. He loves *all* His children the same even though He has not equally distributed spiritual gifts, talents, or intelligence to every person.[43]

There are countless numbers of strongholds that have been raised up against the knowledge of God. The philosophies of this world have affected the way we think, which affects the way we feel, which results in less-than-godly character. Sanctification works the opposite way. It begins by receiving forgiveness, the life of Christ, and a new heart. It continues as we renew our minds by choosing the truth, which in turn affects our emotions and transforms our character.

Positional sanctification assures us that we are new creations in Christ, and we need to appropriate that truth daily by faith. Progressive sanctification is based upon the foundation that we are already children of God, and that the "inner man is being renewed day by day" (2 Corinthians 4:16 NASB). At the same time, we are still contending with the world, the flesh, and the devil. Because we were created in God's image, we have the capacity to choose whom we will serve—the god of this world, or the one and only Creator of all things. Much of progressive sanctification is a struggle to choose between external influences coupled with internal mental strongholds raised up against the knowledge of God, and the internal presence of God coupled with the external help of the body of Christ. Wholeness and true mental health comes when we choose the truth, appropriate it by faith, and walk by the Spirit.

QUESTIONS FOR THOUGHT
AND DISCUSSION

1. Define repentance.

2. Why do we have to renew our minds?

3. How are mental strongholds erected in our minds?

4. What is the nature of temptation?

5. How do the outer person and the inner person work together?

6. Explain the computer analogy of the brain and mind combination.

7. Why is it so important to keep our minds pure?

8. How are we transformed by the renewing of our minds?

CHAPTER EIGHT

The Truth Shall Set You Free

If a man will not think about Christian truth he will not have the blessedness of Christian possession of God. There is no mystery about the road to the sweetness and holiness and power that may belong to a Christian. The only way to win them is to be occupied with the plain truths of God's revelation in Jesus Christ.

ALEXANDER MACLAREN

EVERY CHILD OF GOD IS A DIAMOND in the rough, but we begin our Christian walk looking more like a lump of coal. However, given enough time and pressure, every lump has the potential of becoming a brilliant diamond. If we remove coal from the pressures of the earth and introduce impurities into its chemical composition, it will never achieve its potential. Staying pure and remaining under pressure is what makes a diamond out of coal. Paul wrote, "We also rejoice in our sufferings, because we know that suffering produces perseverance; perseverance, character; and character, hope. And hope does not disappoint us, because God has poured out his love into our hearts by the Holy Spirit, whom he has given us" (Romans 5:3-5).

The Truth Changes Us

There is no such thing as instant maturity. It takes time to be conformed to the image of God, and it happens only if we respond properly to the pressures that inevitably come from living in this fallen world. Scripture teaches that truth brings people to God and then bears fruit in them: "The word of *truth*, the gospel that has come to you...is bearing fruit and growing, just as it has been doing among you since the day you heard it and understood God's grace in all its *truth*" (Colossians 1:5-6). "From the beginning God chose you to be saved through the sanctifying work of the Spirit and through belief in the *truth*" (2 Thessalonians 2:13).

As believers we are to "live by the *truth*" (1 John 1:6), or "practice the *truth*" (NASB). Paul wrote,

> You were taught, with regard to your former way of life, to put off your old self, which is being corrupted by its deceitful desires; to be made new in the attitude of your minds; and to put on the new self, created to be like God in *true* righteousness and holiness (Ephesians 4:22-24).

The latter part of verse 24 is more literally "in righteousness and holiness of the *truth*" (NASB). Many commentators say that truth should be seen as the source of the righteousness and holiness that is being created in the new person. Andrew Lincoln writes,

> The evil desires which characterized the old person sprang from deceit (verse 22). Now by contrast, the virtues which characterize the new person can be said to come from the truth. This truth is ultimately divine reality which has been disclosed in the gospel and the apostolic tradition (cf. 1:13; 4:21).[44]

Growth Involves the Revealing of Our Hearts

Under the New Covenant of grace, we are called to live by faith according to what God says is true in the power of the Holy Spirit. This truth includes the reality of the state of our own heart. In the ultimate sense, the full depth of our hearts cannot be known until the Lord reveals it at His coming. Paul writes,

> I do not even judge myself. My conscience is clear, but that does not make me innocent. It is the Lord who judges me. Therefore judge nothing before the appointed time; wait till the Lord comes. He will bring to light what is hidden in darkness and will expose the motives of men's hearts. At that time each will receive his praise from God (1 Corinthians 4:3-5).

Although we don't have total knowledge of ourselves until the final day, other Bible passages show that the revealing of our hearts also takes place in our present lives. The psalmist prayed, "Search me, O God, and know my heart; test me and know my anxious thoughts. See if there is any offensive way in me, and lead me in the way everlasting" (Psalm 139:23-24). A similar request is found in Psalm 26:2: "Test me, O LORD, and try me, examine my heart and my mind." David was asking God "to prove the state of his mind, and, if it be not as it appears to his consciousness, to make this clear to him."[46]

God also used His prophets to reveal the "secrets" of people's hearts (1 Corinthians 14:24-25). The effect of prophetic revelation, as Charles Hodge explains it, is that a person's "real character and moral state, with regard to which he was before ignorant, are made known to him."[47] The Word of God reveals people's hearts because it

> is living and active. Sharper than any double-edged sword, it penetrates even to dividing soul and spirit, joints and marrow; it judges the thoughts and attitudes of the heart. Nothing in all creation is hidden

from God's sight. Everything is uncovered and laid bare before the eyes of him to whom we must give account (Hebrews 4:12-13).

The process of Christian maturity thus includes God revealing to us unconscious thoughts or the unconscious contents of our heart. Augustine spoke of God revealing the things of a man's heart of which he is unconscious and unaware.[48] The early church father Irenaeus referred to the Spirit revealing in a beneficial way the hidden things of human hearts.[49]

Growth and Transparency

In the words of Gerd Thiessen, Scripture teaches "a conception of an unconscious dimension within the human being. Within this dimension lie not only repressed unconscious deeds but also unconscious plans and motives."[50] With this in mind, one could divide the Christian into four quadrants as follows (as we discuss this diagram, keep in mind that we are talking about character—that is, *who* we are rather than *what* we do):

	You see	You don't see
I see	transparent self	pride
I don't see	blind spots	hidden self

First, there is a part of us that is transparent to all. Second, there is a part of us that we know but others don't. This is the area of conscious cover-up. We all have some aspects of our character and conscious thoughts we don't want others to know. Fear and pride keep us from being transparent. We project an image of ourselves that is not always indicative of who we really are.

Christian growth is inhibited to the degree that we cover ourselves up. Doing so reveals that we are more concerned with how we look to other people than to God. God, however, calls us to "walk in the Light as He Himself is in the Light" (1 John 1:7 NASB), and He wants us to lay aside falsehood and speak the truth with our neighbors because we are members of one another (Ephesians 4:25). "Speaking the truth in love, we are to grow up in all aspects into Him, who is the head, even Christ" (Ephesians 4:15 NASB). Every Christian should make a conscious effort to walk in the light and be a real person by reducing the size of this quadrant of our lives.

We are conscious of everything above the middle line in the diagram above, but there are some things below the line others know about us that we aren't even aware of. These are blind spots, and we all have them. To some degree we can all see the character defects in other people, but we are not supposed to judge them for these defects. We are supposed to accept one another as Christ has accepted us (Romans 15:7). Nothing frees a person more for growth than the love and acceptance of others. (However, *don't* confuse judgment with discipline. Discipline is always based on observed behavior, whereas judgment is related to character.)

The last quadrant in the diagram is that which only God knows. He has total knowledge of us; He even knows how many hairs we have on our heads.

In 1 Corinthians 4:3-5, as we saw, Paul wrote, "It is a very small thing that I may be examined by you, or by any human court; in fact, I do not even examine myself. I am conscious of nothing against myself, yet I am not by this acquitted; but the one who examines me is the Lord" (NASB). We shouldn't be too concerned about what others think of us because the One who examines us is the Lord. Paul had already examined himself and knew of nothing against himself. To his knowledge, he had no unresolved conflicts. He had nothing more to confess, and there was nobody he needed to forgive or ask forgiveness of—however, he was "not by this acquitted."

Paul had reached a healthy plateau in his Christian walk (as we all do at times), and yet he knew he still hadn't arrived. These plateaus are the good times in the sanctification process. We don't feel convicted by anything, and our conscience is clean. (How this relates to Christian growth is shown on the following diagram.)

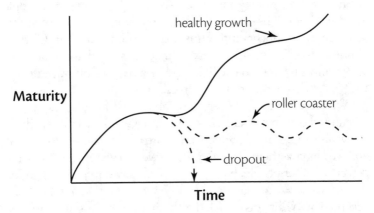

Choose to Grow

No plateau lasts forever. God has ways of letting us know that we are not yet qualified to be a member of the trinity! "Whom the LORD loves He reproves" (Proverbs 3:12 NASB). Reproof should also come when we study His Word if we are in need of correction (2 Timothy 3:16). "He who regards reproof is sensible...He who hates reproof will die" (Proverbs 15:5,10).

There are three basic responses to the reproofs of life. One option is to drop out of the sanctifying process. Those who have dropped out don't come to church, because they don't want to hear the truth. They don't want the conviction, and they don't want to change themselves or their lifestyles. They stay away from anything that will make them feel guilty.

Another option is to hang in there but never grow. These are the classic roller-coaster Christians. They haven't learned from their experiences, so they will have to keep repeating them until they do. They keep going around and around the same mountain, but never grow. Life keeps beating them up, but they are not going to admit they are wrong or seek to grow through the crisis.

In California, there are underground geological faults that are shifting. Seismologists like it when the state experiences small earthquakes. They may shake people up, but little damage is done. However, when no "adjustments" happen for a long time, the scientists begin to predict that the "big one" is coming. The same holds true for us. If we are not making slow, incremental changes in our growth, then the "big one" is coming. Some Christians have to lose their jobs, health, family, friends, and ministry before they own up to their own lack of maturity. Even then, when God exposes their character, it is to get their attention before the final judgment—which is sure to come.

What should we do when God reveals our character defects as we interact with others in this fallen world? We need to own up to our something-less-than-Christlike character. When you react impatiently to others, admit it. Don't blame others or rationalize what you said or did. Just walk in the light by agreeing with God that perfection has still eluded you. Admit what you did, apologize, ask forgiveness, forgive others, or do whatever else Scripture requires of you. A mistake is never a failure unless you fail to learn from it. To stumble and fall is not failure. To stumble and fall again is not failure. Failure comes when you say you were pushed. The reproofs of life don't condemn you as a failure—they just reveal who you really are.

The Battle for the Mind

It seems to some Christians as if they simply aren't able to choose to grow. They struggle and get nowhere. There is an explanation for this, and it involves the mind.

Satan has blinded the minds of unbelievers (2 Corinthians 4:4), and Paul says to believers, "I am afraid that, as the serpent deceived Eve by his craftiness, your minds should be led astray from the simplicity and purity of devotion to Christ" (2 Corinthians 11:3 NASB). Elsewhere, Paul says, "The Spirit clearly says that in later times some will abandon the faith and follow deceiving spirits and things taught by demons" (1 Timothy 4:1). That is happening all over the world. I (Neil) have counseled hundreds of people in many cultures who were struggling with their thoughts and having difficulty concentrating and reading their Bibles. In many cases I have seen, people are hearing "voices." With few exceptions, these people are in a spiritual battle—one that can be resolved through repentance and faith in God.

This battle for the mind is oftentimes being passed off as mental illness. "You have a chemical imbalance," is the common medical explanation given to those who are hearing voices, plagued with negative thoughts, having panic attacks, or struggling with chronic depression. Lacking the advantage of divine revelation, the secular world believes these problems are organic, and medication is prescribed in an attempt to correct them. While it's true that our body chemistry *can* get out of balance, and that hormonal problems *can* cause sickness and disorientation, still, we have to ask questions that raise other possibilities. Questions such as, how can a chemical in the brain produce a personal thought? And how can our neurotransmitters involuntarily and randomly fire in such a way as to create a thought we are opposed to thinking? Is there a *natural* explanation for that? To have a complete answer we must take into account the reality of the spiritual world.

When troubled people hear "voices," what are they actually hearing? The only way we can hear a sound with our ears is to have a physical sound source. Sound waves are a rhythmic compression of air molecules that moves physically through the air and is picked up by our eardrums, which in turn send signals to our brains. But the "voices" or disturbing thoughts that many people "hear" do not come from any kind of physical source. These people are often deemed mentally ill because, from the perspective of naturalistic science, they appear to be out of touch with reality.

Spiritually oppressed people also see things that other people don't, but what are they actually seeing? The only way we can see something with our physical eyes is when light reflects off a material object. The spiritual world, however, doesn't have material substance, so we cannot see a spiritual being with our natural eyes nor hear it with our ears. Paul says that "our struggle is not against flesh and blood, but against the rulers, against the authorities, against the powers of this dark world and against spiritual forces of evil in the heavenly realms" (Ephesians 6:12).

Girding Ourselves with the Truth

If we are to face our struggle successfully, our first line of defense against such spiritual attacks upon our minds is to gird our loins with the truth. The armor of God, like any other armor, stops penetration—yet it cannot be appropriated passively. We have to actively take our place in Christ: "*Put on* the full armor of God, so that when the day of evil comes, you may be able to stand your ground, and after you have done everything, to stand. *Stand firm*" (Ephesians 6:13-14). The way we overcome the father of lies is not by human reasoning, nor by scientific research, but by God's revelation—His truth.

That's why Paul tells us, "From the beginning God chose you to be saved through the sanctifying work of the Spirit and through belief in the *truth*" (2 Thessalonians 2:13). To win the battle for your mind you must also "let the peace of Christ rule in your hearts, since as members of one body you were called to peace. And be thankful" (Colossians 3:15). Rule means to arbitrate or win the battle. You can do this when you "let the word of Christ dwell in you richly as you teach and admonish one another with all wisdom" (verse 16).

Reviewing the Central Truths of Sanctification

Within the Bible are central truths—those that are essential to a believer's understanding and growth. These include

1. the truths related to our salvation, including what God has already done for us and what He will do

2. the imperatives, or commands, that reveal how we as Christians should live

These commands for living are based on *what is already true* about our salvation and the absolute assurance of *what is yet to come* because of our salvation. The beginning point of sanctification is belief in the gospel—believing what God has done for us in salvation. This entails what He has done in the past and what He will yet do for us in the future. Horatius Bonar described it like this:

> The gospel does not command us to do anything in order to obtain life, but it bids us live by that which another has done; and the knowledge of its life-giving truth is not labor but rest—rest of soul, which is the root of all true labor; for in receiving Christ we do not work in order to rest, but we rest in order to work.[51]

By faith, we rest in the finished work of Christ. Faith is a choice to trust in Christ, to believe that He did for us what we couldn't do for ourselves. Our sanctification is dependent upon believing the truth of who we now are in Christ, resting in His finished work, and then living out the implications of this new perspective. God's desire for us in the ongoing process of sanctification is for us to experience in real life who we really are in Christ. This necessitates choosing to believe who we are as children of God on a daily basis. We close with a final encouragement from Scripture:

Since I Am in Christ, by the Grace of God...

Romans 5:1	I have been justified (completely forgiven).
Romans 6:1-6	I died with Christ and died to the power of sin's rule over my life.
Romans 8:1	I am free from condemnation.
1 Corinthians 1:30	I have been placed into Christ by God's doing.
1 Corinthians 2:12	I have received the Spirit of God into my life that I might know the things freely given to me by God.
1 Corinthians 2:16	I have been given the mind of Christ.
1 Corinthians 6:19-20	I have been bought with a price. I am not my own; I belong to God.
2 Corinthians 1:21-22	I have been established, anointed, and sealed by God in Christ.
2 Corinthians 5:14-15	I have died, I no longer live for myself, but for Him.
2 Corinthians 5:21	I have been made righteous.
Galatians 2:20	I have been crucified with Christ and it is no longer I who live, but Christ lives in me (the life I am now living is Christ's life).
Ephesians 1:3	I have been blessed with every spiritual blessing.
Ephesians 1:4	I have been chosen in Christ before the foundation of the world to be holy and without blame before Him.
Ephesians 1:5	I was predestined (determined by God) to be adopted as a son.
Ephesians 1:7-8	I have been redeemed, forgiven, and am a recipient of His lavish grace.

Ephesians 1:13-14	I have been given the Holy Spirit as a pledge (a deposit, or down payment) guaranteeing my inheritance to come.
Ephesians 2:5	I have been made alive together with Christ.
Ephesians 2:6	I have been raised up and seated with Christ in heaven.
Ephesians 2:18	I have direct access to God through the Spirit.
Ephesians 3:12	I may approach God with boldness, freedom, and confidence.
Colossians 1:13	I have been delivered from the domain of darkness (Satan's rule) and transferred to the kingdom of Christ.
Colossians 1:14	I have been redeemed and forgiven of all my sins (the debt against me has been cancelled—see Colossians 2:13-14).
Colossians 1:27	Christ Himself is in me.
Colossians 2:7	I have been firmly rooted in Christ and am now being built up in Him.
Colossians 2:10	I have been made complete in Christ.
Colossians 2:11	I have been spiritually circumcised (my unregenerate nature has been removed).
Colossians 2:12	I have been buried, raised, and made alive with Christ.
Colossians 3:1-4	I have been raised up with Christ. I died with Christ; my life is now hidden with Christ in God. Christ is now *my* life.

2 Timothy 1:7	I have been given a spirit of power, love, and self-discipline.
2 Timothy 1:9	I have been saved and called (set apart) according to God's doing.
Titus 3:5	I have been reborn and renewed by the Holy Spirit.
Hebrews 2:11	I am sanctified and am one with the Sanctifier (Christ), and He is not ashamed to call me His brother.
Hebrews 4:16	I have a right to come boldly before the throne of God (the throne of grace) to find mercy and grace in time of need.
2 Peter 1:4	I have been given exceedingly great and precious promises by God, by which I am a partaker of the divine nature (God's nature).

Questions for Thought
and Discussion

1. Why do you think Christians are reluctant to share with others who they really are?

2. What are the risks and rewards of being vulnerable?

3. What happens if we don't respond properly to the reproofs of life and why don't we?

4. What should we do when life events reveal our immaturity?

5. How can you win the battle for your mind?

6. What are the central truths we all must know in order to grow?

About the
Steps to Freedom in Christ

FREEDOM IN CHRIST MINISTRIES HAS BEEN helping people all over the world resolve personal and spiritual conflicts through genuine repentance and faith in God. The discipleship counseling tool we use is titled the Steps to Freedom in Christ. (The Steps can be purchased in book form from any Christian bookstore or from the home office of Freedom in Christ Ministries. They are also found in Neil's book *The Bondage Breaker*.)

Seven Areas of Confession and Repentance

Scripture reveals seven categories of sins and iniquities that need to be confessed and repented of if a Christian hopes to have an intimate relationship with God. Through the Steps to Freedom in Christ, believers petition God to show them what they need to repent of in each of these areas.

First, *we should confess and renounce any involvement with false prophets and teachers, as well as any involvement with cults or the occult.* "He who conceals his sins does not prosper, but whoever confesses and renounces them finds mercy" (Proverbs 28:13 NIV). God does not take false teachers and false guidance lightly. In the Old Testament, false teachers were to be put to death (see

Deuteronomy 13:5), and there were serious consequences for those who consulted them: "I will set my face against the person who turns to mediums and spiritists to prostitute himself by following them, and I will cut him off from his people" (Leviticus 20:6 NIV). Obviously we are not going to have an effective prayer time if God is cutting us off from Him and His people.

Second, *we are warned not to be deceived*. Deceived people are living in bondage to the lies they believe, and believing those lies seriously affects their walk with God. If Christians are paying attention to deceiving spirits, they are not paying attention to God. If they believe they need to defend themselves, they are not trusting Christ to be their defense. Certainly, no believer can instantly renew his or her mind, tear down mental strongholds, and overcome old defense mechanisms. But the process of renewing our minds won't even begin unless we are aware of our false beliefs and defenses—and God is willing to reveal them to us if we ask.

Third, *we need to forgive from our hearts as Christ has forgiven us*. We can't have an intimate relationship with God and hold bitterness in our hearts. Jesus said that our heavenly Father would turn us over to the torturers if we don't forgive (Matthew 18:34-35). It is hard to hear from God if our minds are tormented by thoughts about other people who have hurt us. So when we are trying to pray to God and our minds are plagued by thoughts of the injustices done to us by other people, we can know that God is allowing the mental torment so we will be driven to forgive others and seek forgiveness. In fact, some of these kinds of thoughts we struggle with are coming from Satan. Paul urges us to forgive, because we are not ignorant of Satan's schemes (2 Corinthians 2:11).*

---

* The Greek word translated as "schemes" in this verse is *noema*. Elsewhere in 2 Corinthians it is translated as "thought" (10:5) or "minds" (4:4; 11:3).

When I encourage people to pray and ask God to reveal to their minds who they need to forgive, God does it. Sometimes people pray and then say there is nobody they need to forgive. When that happens, I just ask them to share with me the names that are coming to their minds—and out will come several names of people they need to forgive. Some may be hardening their hearts because they would rather seek revenge. Others are afraid to face their pain, so they live in denial or try to shove it down into the unconscious...but God is trying to bring the pain to the surface so they can let it go by forgiving.

Fourth, *we have to come to terms with our pride.* You cannot have a close relationship with God if He is opposed to you, but if you humbly ask, God will show you how prideful you have been. Notice how James connects pride with the world, flesh, and the devil:

> You ask and do not receive, because you ask with wrong motives, so that you may spend it on your own pleasures. You adulteresses, do you not know that friendship with the world is hostility toward God? Therefore whoever wishes to be a friend of the world makes himself an enemy of God. Or do you think that the Scripture speaks to no purpose: "He jealously desires the Spirit which He has made to dwell in us?" But He gives a greater grace. Therefore it says, "God is opposed to the proud, but gives grace to the humble" (4:3-7).

We can't pray by the Spirit and be prideful.

Fifth, *we can't pray by the Spirit and be rebellious either.* Rebellion is as the sin of witchcraft and insubordination is as iniquity and idolatry (see 1 Samuel 15:23). God requires that all His children submit to governing authorities (Romans 13:1-7), parents (Ephesians 6:1-3), spouses (1 Peter 3:1-7; Ephesians 5:21-25), employers (1 Peter 2:18-23), church leaders (Hebrews 13:17), and God Himself (Daniel 9:5,9).

What happens in our courts of law when a rebellious prisoner approaches the bench disrespectfully? He is thrown out of court for contempt. The judge will not even hear from the accused—and neither will our heavenly Father hear from us in prayer if we approach Him disrespectfully and disobey His commands to submit to His established authority. If we ask Him, He will reveal our rebelliousness.

Sixth, *we can't expect God to hear our prayers if we are living in sin*. Rest assured He knows our sins and will bring conviction, so we aren't fooling anyone when we try to hide them. If they have never been acknowledged, these issues will plague our minds when we try to pray. That is what David tried to do, and he suffered for it. Finally, he turned to God—and later he recorded his experience in Psalm 32:1-6:

> How blessed is he whose transgression is forgiven, whose sin is covered! How blessed is the man to whom the Lord does not impute iniquity, and in whose spirit there is no deceit!
>
> When I kept silent about my sin, my body wasted away through my groaning all day long. For day and night Your hand was heavy upon me; my vitality was drained away as with the fever heat of summer...I acknowledged my sin to You, and my iniquity I did not hide; I said, "I will confess my transgressions to the LORD"; and You forgave the guilt of my sin... Therefore, let everyone who is godly pray to You in a time when You may be found; surely in a flood of great waters they will not reach him.

Finally, *we cannot pray effectively if we continue in the sins of our ancestors*. Peter urged us,

> If you address as Father the One who impartially judges according to each one's work, conduct yourselves in fear during the time of your stay on earth; knowing that you were not redeemed with perishable things like silver or gold from *your futile way of life inherited from your forefathers*, but with precious blood, as of a lamb unblemished and spotless, the blood of Christ (1 Peter 1:17-19).

Sometimes we can be torn between our natural heritage and our spiritual heritage. Jesus is the sword that divides the family if our earthly parents and siblings are at odds with our heavenly Father. Our Savior said, "He who loves father or mother more than me is not worthy of Me; and he who loves son or daughter more than Me is not worthy of Me. And he who does not take his cross and follow after Me is not worthy of Me" (Matthew 10:37-38). Any attempt to hold a marriage or family together at the expense of our relationship with our heavenly Father is not in His plan. Compromising our faith to save a marriage doesn't work. The marriage won't be any good—and neither will our walk with God.

Under the Old Covenant, the Israelites confessed their sins and the sins of their fathers. This was necessary because people have a tendency to live according to how they have been taught. As Jesus noted, "A pupil is not above his teacher; but everyone, after he has been fully trained, will be like his teacher" (Luke 6:40). Nobody had more influence on us in our first five years than our parents, and unless we repent, we will live out the beliefs and values we have been taught...or caught from the environment of our homes. We are never guilty of our parents' sins, but because all parents have sinned, we have picked up some of their attitudes and actions that are not consistent with our Christianity.

The Effectiveness of the Steps

There have been several exploratory studies that have shown promising results regarding the effectiveness of the Steps. Judith King, a Christian therapist, did three pilot studies in 1996 on participants who attended a "Living Free in Christ" conference. They were given an opportunity to process the Steps at the end of the conference. The first study involved 30 participants who took a ten-item questionnaire before completing the Steps. The questionnaire was re-administered three months after their participation. The questionnaire assessed for levels of depression, anxiety, inner conflict, tormenting thoughts, and addictive behaviors. The second study involved 55 participants, and the third involved 21 participants, who were tested in the same way. The following table illustrates the percentage of improvement for each category.

	Pilot Study 1	Pilot Study 2	Pilot Study 3
Depression	64%	47%	52%
Anxiety	58%	44%	47%
Inner Conflict	63%	51%	48%
Tormenting Thoughts	82%	58%	57%
Addictive Behavior	52%	43%	39%

Further research was conducted by doctoral students at Regent University under the supervision of Dr. Fernando Garzon, Doctor of Psychology, on the message and method of Freedom in Christ Ministries. Most people attending a "Living Free in Christ" conference can work through the repentance process on their own using the Steps to Freedom in Christ.

About 15 percent can't, because of difficulties they have experienced. A personal session is offered them with a trained encourager. At two seminars, these people were given a pre-test before a session of going through the Steps, and a post-test three months later. Here are the results, given in percentage of improvement:

	Oklahoma City, Oklahoma, Seminar	Tyler, Texas, Seminar
Depression	44%	57%
Anxiety	45%	54%
Fear	48%	49%
Anger	36%	55%
Tormenting Thoughts	51%	50%
Negative Habits	48%	53%
Sense of Self-Worth	52%	56%

Resolving personal and spiritual conflicts through repentance and faith in God establishes Christians alive and free in Christ. Once firmly rooted in Christ, they are free to grow. (To learn how to help people with the Steps, see Neil's book *Discipleship Counseling*—Regal Books, 2003.)

Our heavenly Father wants all His children to live free and productive lives in Christ. May the good Lord enable you to be all that He created you to be—then you can become an instrument in His hands to set the captives free and bind up the brokenhearted.

Notes

1. Adapted from Neil T. Anderson, *Who I Am in Christ* (Ventura, CA: Regal Books, 2001), pp. 56-58. ©2001 Gospel Light/Regal Books, Ventura, CA 93003. Used by Permission.

2. George Fohrer, "σώζω κτλ.," *Theological Dictionary of the New Testament*, ed. Gerhard Friedrich, vol. 7 (Grand Rapids, MI: Eerdmans, 1971), p. 973.

3. Charles Hodge, *The Way of Life*, ed. Mark A. Noll (Mahwah, NJ: Paulist Press, 1987), pp. 217-218.

4. See the article by Karl Heinrich Rengstorf in the *Theological Dictionary of the New Testament*, ed. Gerhard Kittel, vol. 1 (Grand Rapids, MI: Eerdmans, 1964), pp. 327-328; and George W. Knight, *The Pastoral Epistles* (Grand Rapids, MI: Eerdmans, 1992), p. 101.

5. Simon J. Kistemaker, *James and I–III John* (Grand Rapids, MI: Baker, 1986), p. 140.

6. Louis Berkhof, *Systematic Theology* (Grand Rapids, MI: Eerdmans, 1941), p. 527.

7. J.I. Packer, *Rediscovering Holiness* (Ann Arbor, MI: Servant Publications, 1992), p. 26.

8. Chris Brain and Robert Warren, "Why Revival Really Tarries—Holiness," *Renewal* (June 1991), p. 35; cited by Packer, pp. 27-28.

9. Horatius Bonar, *God's Way of Holiness* (New York: Robert Carter & Brothers, 1865), p. 23.

10. David Needham, *Alive for the First Time* (Sisters, OR: Multnomah Books, 1995), p. 34.

11. The being "made righteous" in this verse may refer to the future final ratification of the righteous standing of the believer. But whether present or future, our justification is always finally based on the obedience or righteousness of Christ and not on our own works of obedience.

12. Adapted from Neil T. Anderson, *Living Free in Christ* (Ventura, CA: Regal Books, 1993) pp. 39-40. Used by Permission.

13. See John Murray, "Definitive Sanctification" and "The Agency in Definitive Sanctification" in *Collected Writings of John Murray*, vol. 2 (Carlisle, PA: Banner of Truth Trust, 1977), pp. 227-293.

14. Bonar, p. 52.

15. Adapted from Neil T. Anderson, *Who I Am in Christ* (Ventura, CA: Regal Books, 2001). ©2001 Gospel Light/Regal Books, Ventura, CA 93003. Used by Permission.

16. The other uses of this term (John 3:31; 19:11,23) all carry the meaning of "from above." John tends to describe man's birth in terms of its origin and not simply the idea of another birth. Birth is either from God or the flesh (see John 1:13; 1 John 2:29; 3:9; 4:7; 5:18).

17. E.K. Simpson and F.F. Bruce, *Commentary on the Epistles to the Ephesians and the Colossians* (Grand Rapids, MI: Eerdmans, 1957), p. 273.

18. Peter T. O'Brien, "Colossians, Philemon," *Word Biblical Commentary*, vol. 44 (Waco, TX: Word Books, 1982), pp. 27-28.

19. Robert Jewett, *Paul's Anthropological Terms* (Leiden, The Netherlands: E.J. Brill, 1971), p. 313. Compare also Laidlaw's description of the heart as "the workplace for the personal appropriation and assimilation of every influence" (John Laidlaw, *The Bible Doctrine of Man* [Edinburgh: T. & T. Clark, 1895], p. 122).

20. D.A. Carson, "Matthew," in *The Expositor's Bible Commentary*, ed. Frank E. Gaebelein, vol. 8 (Grand Rapids, MI: Zondervan, 1984), p. 177.

21. John Calvin, *The Institutes of the Christian Religion*, II, iii, 6.

22. John Stott, *God's Good News for the World* (Downers Grove, IL: InterVarsity Press, 1994), p. 187.

23. Stott, p. 187.

24. H. Wheeler Robinson, *The Christian Doctrine of Man* (Edinburgh: T. & T. Clark, 1926), p. 22. The same concept of the heart carries over into the New Testament.

25. The "putting off" and "putting on" in Ephesians 4:22-24 can also be interpreted like Romans 6:6 and Colossians 3:9-10—in the sense that these actions have already taken place in the past. The Greek infinitives translated "to put off" (verse 22) and "to put on" (verse 24) can be understood as "explanatory infinitives" expressing the content and result of that which the believers had been "taught" in the past (verse 21)—"you were taught that you have put off…" (Compare Harold W. Hoehner, *Ephesians: An Exegetical Commentary* [Grand Rapids, MI: Baker, 2003], pp. 600ff).

26. Andrew T. Lincoln, "Ephesians," *Word Biblical Commentary*, vol. 42 (Dallas, TX: Word Books, 1990), pp. 285-286.

27. Roy A. Harrisville, *Romans*, cited by James D.G. Dunn, "Romans 9-16," *Word Biblical Commentary*, vol. 38B (Dallas, TX: Word Books), p. 712.

28. Richard N. Longenecker, "Galatians," *Word Biblical Commentary*, vol. 41 (Dallas, TX: Word Books, 1990), p. 156.

29. Glenn E. Hinson, "The Contemplative View," in *Christian Spirituality*, ed. Donald L. Alexander (Downers Grove, IL: InterVarsity Press, 1988), p. 177.

30. Peter Kreeft, *The God Who Loves You* (Ann Arbor, MI: Servant Books, 1988), pp. 140-141.

31. Kreeft, p. 112.

32. Henry Scougal, *The Life of God in the Soul of Man* (Philadelphia: Westminster Press, 1948), p. 38.

33. Calvin, III, iii, 11.

34. Calvin, III, iii, 10.

35. Neil T. Anderson, *Victory Over the Darkness* (Ventura, CA: Regal Books, 2000), pp. 51-52. ©2000 Gospel Light/Regal Books, Ventura, CA 93003. Used by Permission.

36. Longenecker, p. 93.

37. Robert C. Tannehill, *Dying and Rising with Christ* (Berlin: Alfred Töpelmann, 1967), p. 19.

38. Moses Silva, *Philippians* (Grand Rapids, MI: Baker Book House, 1992), p. 139.

39. John Murray, *Redemption: Accomplished and Applied* (London: Banner of Truth, 1961), pp. 148-149.

40. As quoted in Lincoln, p. 116.

41. Robert Durback, ed., *Seed of Hope: A Henri Nouwen Reader* (New York: Bantam Books, 1990), p. 197.

42. For a more complete explanation of how to understand and resolve chemical addictions and sexual bondages in Christ, see Neil's books *Overcoming Addictive Behavior* (Regal Books, 2003) and *Finding Freedom in a Sex-Obsessed World* (Harvest House Publishers, 2004).

43. For more information, see Neil's book *Overcoming a Negative Self-Image* (Regal Books, 2003).

44. Lincoln, p. 288.

45. To learn more about what it means to live by faith see Neil's book, *Overcoming Doubt* (Regal Books, 2003).

46. Franz Delitzsch, *Biblical Commentary on the Psalms*, vol. 1 (Grand Rapids, MI: Eerdmans, 1959), p. 350.

47. Charles Hodge, *An Exposition of the First Epistle to the Corinthians* (Grand Rapids, MI: Eerdmans, 1953), p. 298.

48. William Watts, *St. Augustine's Confessions*, vol. 2 (Cambridge, MA: Harvard University Press, 1912), p. 85.

49. A. Roberts and J. Donaldson, *Ante-Nicene Fathers*, 1:531.

50. Gerd Thiessen, *Psychological Aspects of Pauline Theology* (Philadelphia: Fortress, 1983), p. 66.

51. Bonar, pp. 41-42.

Resources from Freedom in Christ Ministries and Neil T. Anderson

Core Message and Resources

- *The Bondage Breaker*® (Harvest House). Study guide and audiobook also available. This book explains spiritual warfare, what your protection is, ways that you are vulnerable, and how you can live a liberated life in Christ. Well over one million copies in print.

- *Victory Over the Darkness* with study guide, audiobook, and videos (Regal Books). Explains who you are in Christ, how you walk by faith, how your mind and emotions function, and how to relate to one another in Christ. Well over one million copies in print.

- *Breaking Through to Spiritual Maturity* (Regal Books). A curriculum for teaching the basic message of Freedom in Christ Ministries.

- *Discipleship Counseling* with videos (Regal Books). Discipleship and counseling integrated practically with theology and psychology to help Christians resolve personal and spiritual conflicts through repentance.

- *Steps to Freedom in Christ* and interactive video (Regal Books). This discipleship counseling tool helps Christians resolve their personal and spiritual conflicts.

The Bondage Breaker® **Series** (Harvest House). Truth from the Word of God on specific issues—to bring you help and freedom in your life.

- *Praying by the Power of the Spirit*
- *Finding God's Will in Spiritually Deceptive Times*
- *Finding Freedom in a Sex-Obsessed World*
- *Unleashing God's Power in You* (with Robert Saucy)

Resources on Specific Issues

- *Getting Anger Under Control* with Rich Miller (Harvest House). Exposes the basis for anger and shows how you can control it.

- *Freedom from Fear* with Rich Miller (Harvest House). Discusses fear, anxiety, and anxiety disorders, revealing how you can be free from them.

- *Daily in Christ* (Harvest House). This popular daily devotional will encourage, motivate, and challenge you to experience the reality of *Christ in you*.

- *Breaking the Bondage of Legalism* with Rich Miller and Paul Travis (Harvest House). An exposure and explanation of legalism, the guilt and shame it brings, and how you can overcome it.

- *Battle Plan for Spiritual Warfare.* Joe Wasmond and Rich Miller (Harvest House). Joe Wasmond's real-life battle experiences frame powerful messages about biblical strategies for spiritual warfare.

- *God's Power at Work in You* with Dr. Robert Saucy (Harvest House). A thorough analysis of sanctification, along with practical instruction on how you can grow in Christ.
- *A Way of Escape* (Harvest House). Exposes the bondage of sexual strongholds and shows you how they can be torn down in Christ.
- *The Seduction of Our Children* with Steve Russo (Harvest House). Reveals how you as a parent can be equipped to help teens.
- *Who I Am in Christ* (Regal Books). How He meets your deepest needs.
- *Freedom from Addiction* with Mike Quarles (Regal Books).
- *One Day at a Time* with Mike Quarles (Regal Books).
- *The Christ-Centered Marriage* with Dr. Charles Mylander (Regal Books).
- *The Spiritual Protection of Our Children* with Peter and Sue Vander Hook (Regal Books).
- *Leading Teens to Freedom in Christ* with Rich Miller (Regal Books).
- *Finding Hope Again* with Hal Baumchen (Regal Books). Depression and how to overcome it.
- *Released from Bondage* with Judy King and Dr. Fernando Garzon (Thomas Nelson).
- *Freedom in Christ Bible* (Zondervan). A one-year discipleship study with notes in the Bible.
- *Blessed Are the Peacemakers* with Dr. Charles Mylander (Regal Books).
- *A Biblical Guide to Alternative Medicine* with Dr. Michael Jacobson (Regal Books).
- *Setting Your Church Free* with Dr. Charles Mylander (Regal Books).
- *Christ-Centered Therapy* with Dr. Terry and Julie Zuehlke (Zondervan).

The Victory Over the Darkness Series (Regal Books)
- *Overcoming a Negative Self-Image* with Dave Park
- *Overcoming Addictive Behavior* with Mike Quarles
- *Overcoming Doubt*
- *Overcoming Depression*

Contact information for Freedom in Christ Ministries:
9051 Executive Park Drive, Suite 503
Knoxville, TN 37923
Telephone: (865) 342-4000
E-mail: info@ficm.org • Web site: www.ficm.org